MW00579875

Gardens of Heaven and Earth

Gardens of Heaven and Earth

Kristin King

The Swedenborg Society
Swedenborg House
20-21 Bloomsbury Way
London WC1A 2TH

2011

Published by:
The Swedenborg Society
Swedenborg House
20-21 Bloomsbury Way
London WC1A 2TH

© 2011, The Swedenborg Society

Donald Moorhead's drawing of Swedenborg's garden
was first published in *The New Philosophy*, 1953,
and is reproduced by permission of
the Swedenborg Scientific Association.

Typeset at Swedenborg House.
Printed by T J International, Padstow.
Book and cover design: Stephen McNeilly

ISBN: 978-0-85448-169-9
British Library Cataloguing-in-Publication Data.
A catalogue record for this book is available
from the British Library.

for JSR,
my favourite garden,
in every season

Table of Contents

Acknowledgements

I am grateful to the Academy of the New Church Research Committee for its encouragement and generous support of several stages of research; to Bryn Athyn College for release time to bring this book to completion; and to my colleagues for many inspiring conversations.

Thank you as well to Stephen McNeilly and the editorial team of the Swedenborg Society at Swedenborg House, particularly David Lister and Josephine Appelgren, who contributed well-honed proofreading skills. Finally, I am much indebted to James Wilson for his deft and patient guidance of the publication process.

Swedenborg: Life and Works

1688   January 29, born Emanuel Swedberg.

1696   Emanuel's mother, Sara Behm, dies June 17.

1709   Emanuel graduates from Uppsala University.

1710   First trip abroad.

1714   Finishes designs of various inventions, including an airplane and submarine.

1716   Swedenborg publishes the first issues of the scientific journal *Daedalus Hyperboreus*.

1719   Family ennoblement and change of name to Swedenborg.

1723   Swedenborg's appointment as extraordinary assessor on the Board of Mines is recognized.

1734   Publishes his philosophical and scientific work *The Principia*.

1740-1   Publishes *The Economy of the Animal Kingdom*.

1735   Emanuel's father, Bishop Jesper Swedberg, dies.

1743-4   First addressed by a spirit. Writes his *Journal of Dreams*.

1747   Resigns from Board of Mines.

1749-56   Publishes his eight-volume biblical exegesis *Arcana Caelestia*.

1757   Writes of a 'last judgment' in the spirit world.

1758   Whilst in London, Swedenborg publishes *The Worlds in Space*; *Heaven and Hell*; *The Last Judgment*; *The New Jerusalem*; and *The White Horse*.

1763   Publishes *The Doctrine of the Lord*; *The Doctrine of the Sacred Scripture*; *The Doctrine of Life*; *The Doctrine of Faith*; *Continuation on the Last Judgment*; and *Divine Love and Wisdom*.

1764   Publishes *Divine Providence*.

1766   Publishes *The Apocalyspe Revealed*. Immanuel Kant publishes his attack on Swedenborg entitled *Dreams of a Spirit Seer*.

1768   Publishes *Conjugial Love*.

1769   Publishes *A Brief Exposition* and *The Interaction of the Soul and Body*.

1770   Swedenborg makes an appeal to King Adolf Frederik regarding the controversy in Sweden surrounding his *Conjugial Love*.

1771   Publishes *The True Christian Religion*. In the same year he suffers a stroke but partially recovers.

1772   Writes to John Wesley. On Sunday, March 29, Swedenborg dies.

Introduction

Overview

The following essay looks at three areas: first, the correspondence or spiritual meaning of gardens in the natural world and in the Bible; second, gardens in heaven as depicted in the work of Emanuel Swedenborg, an eighteenth-century Swede; and third, a cursory view of gardens in the past, ending with Swedenborg's own modest garden. The term 'correspondence' here is key.[1]

Fifty-five years into a life of active engagement with science, philosophy and civil service,[2] Swedenborg claimed to have broken through to a spiritual world where for the remainder of his twenty-nine years he travelled, bore witness, conversed and taught, all the while continuing his life in the natural world and recording his experiences for posterity. With some important exceptions, posterity has largely ignored Swedenborg, keeping a wary distance from a writer whose claims and assertions appear eccentric, even unhinged, to many readers. But patient and curious readers can also find something comforting and stable in Swedenborg's methodical and calm explorations of matter and spirit, something inspiring in his awareness and consistency. This study is not an apology for a Swedenborgian world view. Rather, it is an expression of appreciation for the thoughts and images Swedenborg puts in play through writing about two worlds—a natural world of matter, and a spiritual world of substance—and about the meaning of gardens on multiple levels.

Earthly gardens, textual gardens and heavenly gardens share some common ground. Swedenborg explains that the correspondence or spiritual meaning of gardens in the Word [3] and in the world arises from the spiritual phenomenon that angels' affections and thoughts manifest themselves as gardens in heaven. Since natural reality flows from spiritual reality, as Swedenborg asserts, we have gardens here on earth because angels have gardens in heaven. Not only do earthly gardens derive from spiritual realities but spiritual gardens can reflect new things on earth, as Swedenborg discovered once when talking with angel women in a heavenly rose garden: 'Such [gardens]', the women said of the bands of colour fanning out around them, 'are created by the Lord in a moment, and they represent something new on earth'. [4] Swedenborg spent time in natural and spiritual gardens and wrote about their meaning. Looking at what he says about gardens, and what he learns and teaches while in them, can open new ways to appreciate and experience our own gardens, whether physical, metaphorical or spiritual.

This study does not attempt to pin down in an objective way what gardens mean. Experts do not agree on how to define or describe what constitutes a garden, let alone its purpose. As an art form, gardening has been in constant flux over the ages. Even a seemingly simple garden does not hold still from day to day, or season to season, thus further challenging the effort to categorize and define them. [5] Instead of defining or assigning meaning to these ongoing performances called 'gardens', this study tries to stir appreciation, from a Swedenborgian perspective, for the ways gardens can engage and inspire us to root ourselves in a natural world in order to grow simultaneously in a spiritual one.

Each of the three main topics addressed in this study—garden correspondences, gardens in heaven and gardens in history—offers insights about human nature. First, the correspondence of gardens in the Word teaches about the process of regeneration by which the individual seeks to recover the garden context lost by the species. Second, a view of Swedenborg's descriptions of heaven's gardens teaches something about the landscapes there, slightly more about the nature of angels, and most of all about the limits of human language and of Swedenborg's attention to visual detail. There were things Swedenborg *could not* describe in human language, but also things he chose not to describe. Third, a sweeping view of garden history reveals a 6,000-year effort to find an aesthetic relationship with the natural world. If indeed, as Swedenborg claims, newcomers to heaven initially experience their surroundings much as they experienced them in the world, then this third view of the different faces of gardening over centuries and across continents provides a glimpse of the infinite variety of heaven's horticulture.

Thresholds

Gardens serve as symbolic thresholds between natural and spiritual worlds. Throughout recorded history, from Sumerian gardens of 6,000 years ago to Zen retreats of the modern era, people have built gardens, in part, to reflect heaven or the desire for spiritual transcendence. One of the oldest words for garden—*paradise*—is a synonym for heaven in many cultures. Penelope Hobhouse points to the use of the word *paradise* in early translations of the Old Testament and to its association with the Garden of Eden in both Jewish and Christian traditions. [6] In Persian the word *paradise* is connected to *pairi*, meaning 'around', and *diz*, meaning 'form', thus suggesting a space that is set apart or protected from the surrounding environment. The Bagh-i-Babur, a 'paradise garden' laid out by the founder of the Mughal dynasty on the edge of modern Kabul, Afghanistan, is just one of numerous examples of gardens whose purpose was to 'represent the idea of heaven on earth.'[7] So deeply implanted is this concept of heaven as a garden that when people die and enter spiritual life, Swedenborg tells us, they are taken to gardens as part of their orientation.[8] Swedenborg frequently meditated in and on his earthly garden as a threshold to spiritual travel, and once transported to another realm, he often learned and taught in gardens. Gardens in heaven, as Swedenborg describes them, manifest angels' inner life, specifically the rational level of the mind, which is itself a threshold: 'in between the internal [person] and the external [person]'.[9] Thus we can view gardens as thresholds in a number of ways: on earth we plant gardens to mirror heaven; after death we enter heaven through garden experiences; and once settled in heavenly communities, our inner life manifests itself as a garden, constantly changing to reflect our state of mind and heart.

A paucity of detail—what not to expect

Given Swedenborg's attention to the symbolic value of gardens as thresholds between inner and outer life and between heaven and earth, we might expect that close examination of heavenly gardens would open a window on spiritual life and on the quality of the angels who live there. Swedenborg's descriptions, however, disappoint that expectation. Often hesitant or incomplete, these descriptions culminate in mental abstractions rather than tangible details. In describing a garden in heaven Swedenborg will frequently begin with enthusiasm about the beauty of the place but then take a cerebral turn into what the garden represents. He seems rigorously oblivious to external details: 'The pleasant and the beautiful things of these paradises are not what affect the beholder', he insists, 'but the celestial spiritual things that live in them'. [10] This focus in heaven on the meaning rather than the container resembles the focus of the most ancient people, [11] who similarly saw *through* external objects to spiritual meaning: 'they thought not at all of the objects', Swedenborg testifies, 'but only of the things they meant and represented, which to them were most delightful, for they were such things as exist in heaven, from which they behold the Lord Himself'. [12] Angels too practise this sort of vision by which they see the deeper reality behind objects. Whereas newcomers to heaven 'normally make first of all for the paradise gardens', and are subsequently dumbfounded by the inexpressible beauty, the angels see the gardens quite differently: 'It is not the gardens that delight them but [. . .] the celestial and spiritual things that give rise to them'. [13] Heavenly gardens seem then to deflect attention as quickly as they attract it. Similarly, Swedenborg attests throughout his writing to the existence of vibrant details of heavenly life and the heightening of all sensual experience there, including sexuality, but the details are always subordinated to purposes that transcend sensual pleasure alone. His descriptions of hell and evil spirits, on the other hand, fester with rank detail, perhaps because hell manifests the *failure* to subordinate lower loves to higher ones, loves of the body and self to love of others and community.

The angels, as Swedenborg experiences them, are certainly not oblivious to their garden surroundings. The 'vast' and 'breath-taking' gardens of heaven are presented so keenly before their eyes that they 'not merely see them but even perceive the details far more vividly than the sight of the eye can take such things in on earth'. [14] But these vivid details are not what matter. The beautiful gardens, whose lush appearance and exotic scents lie well beyond our earthly imagination and senses, are still as nothing compared to the heavenly ideas that give rise to them. The angels experience the garden *behind* the garden, and it is these *inner* gardens that captivate Swedenborg as well.

As curious, sensual readers, our quest to see and experience the gardens of heaven meets the recurring obstacle of Swedenborg's and the angels' apparent disinterest in external detail. No sooner do these heavenly gardens register sensorially than they transform, in Swedenborg's highly spiritual consciousness, to thought. We learn what the change signifies but are left largely to wonder about the colour, shape, texture and scent of these miraculous gardens and groves. Anchored as we are in our senses and in earthly life, we might like to linger on the threshold, in the sensual experience of heavenly gardens. The instructive level of the text, however, shuttles us quickly behind the surface to focus exclusively on signification. The signification as relayed by Swedenborg is, of course, only a second-hand *telling* of meaning, not the actual experience. An actual experience of correspondence, I imagine, is a sensory stimulation——the scent of a flower, liquid note of a bird, or texture of bark——so pouring through our spirit that meaning falls like rain on parched thought. It is not that one thing merely points to another thing elsewhere but that 'celestial-spiritual elements [. . .] *live within*' the external objects. [15] Poets, with their faith in the spiritual power of language, seem to grasp the living experience of correspondence, which must be something like William Blake finding eternity in a wild flower, Emily Dickinson locating sacred ritual in slanted light, or Henry David Thoreau discovering the ancient world in the play of sunlight and water on speckled trout. The 'inscape' of Gerard Manley Hopkins, epiphanies of James Joyce and glazed wheelbarrows of William Carlos Williams, testify to a natural world charged with spiritual life, if we have sufficient imagination to open the door.

Swedenborg's tendency to bypass sensual impressions of gardens perhaps intends to protect us from getting waylaid by the senses. At times Swedenborg sounds almost cavalier about the insignificance of external detail, as when he dismisses the importance of an exact translation for a word such as *dudaim*:

> Translators do not know what dudaim were. They all think that they were fruits or flowers and each translator uses a name that fits in with his particular ideas of what dudaim were. But knowledge of what kind of fruit or flower they were is unimportant. All that one needs to know is that among the ancients who belonged to the Church all fruits and flowers had spiritual meanings, for the ancients knew that the whole natural order was a theatre representative of the Lord's kingdom [...]. They knew that all things in its three kingdoms were representative, and that every individual thing, and so also every particular kind of fruit or flower, represented some specific thing in the spiritual world. [16]

Although for the ancient people particular fruits or flowers represented specific things, for the reader it is apparently sufficient to know this general fact and not the identity of the plants. Swedenborg emphasizes the linguistic significance of the *word*, not its referential power to recall a specific flower: 'As regards "dudaim" meaning for them the conjugial [17] element present in good and in truth', Swedenborg goes on to argue, 'this may be seen from the train of thought in the internal sense here, and also from the derivation of that word in the original language. For dudaim is derived from the word *dudim* which means loves and being joined together by means of these'. [18] Ironically, Swedenborg here seems trapped in language, drawing attention to linguistic roots over referential power. Although Swedenborg refers to an 'original' language (Hebrew), at a more basic level the original language of the most ancient people, from whom the knowledge of correspondence was passed down, was not any particular linguistic system of signs but a flow of meaning through natural objects—flowers and oak trees, or bird flight printed on air—and communication was affected by facial expression, especially around the eyes and mouth. [19] Verbal language and writing came later, conveying as second-hand knowledge what had been lost as first-hand experience. It is surprising that Swedenborg's scientific background, connection to the great botanist Linnaeus, and broad interests in horticulture and gardening did not lead him to make more careful accounts of the flora and fauna of heaven. Some other imperative shaped his account.

Far from lingering in descriptive detail when he is in heavenly gardens, Swedenborg seems to operate in a heightened eighteenth-century cerebral mode, as if on guard against the senses. At least he seems this way when he records his spiritual experiences. In his earthly garden, on the other hand, he was relaxed, pottering, at times playful. The few accounts of him in his garden describe him as approachable and kind, eager to share his garden with visitors and well-mannered children. [20] On one occasion, Swedenborg mistakenly assumed that a learned visitor had come to ramble with him in his garden, when in fact he had come to discuss Swedenborg's books and ideas. [21] The garden in Stockholm was a place in which to stroll, meditate, dig in the earth and glean inspiration for mental labours. By way of contrast, the gardens in heaven seem insubstantial, almost mirage-like, at least as they come to us through Swedenborg.

Terminology

Swedenborg uses a variety of words in his original Latin texts to designate gardens, groves and parks, from *floretum* to *hortus* to *arboretum* to *paradisus*. As with all translation, we cannot know absolutely what Swedenborg meant by the words he used. To do so, we would need to live inside his mind and his times. And even then we would perhaps surrender our demand for precision and clarity to embrace instead an appreciation for how tirelessly Swedenborg struggled to find earthbound words to convey spiritual reality. However, our looking at the gardens of Swedenborg's day and of previous times can give us at least some sense of what images he might have had in mind as he used garden terms in his descriptions of heaven, which he did over 1,200 times in his published theological works.

I use the word *garden* loosely throughout this study to designate plants arranged in relationship to one another for aesthetic effect and for the production of flowers. I do not include the broad realm of agriculture, which concerns food production primarily and aesthetic appeal incidentally, though some would argue that food production does not negate aesthetic appeal. [22] Nor do I explore the many passages in Swedenborg's work that mention individual plants and trees, often as powerful illustrations of a person's spiritual growth and regeneration. Instead, this study focuses on plants growing in relation to one another or to a landscape in order to show how the ordering of plants—consciously by human hands, unconsciously by angelic hearts, or omnisciently by divine design—creates a text for us to read, and more importantly, to be moved by.

Landscapes

Three landscapes are particularly important in this study. There are linguistic landscapes—the textual references to gardens in the Bible, the correspondence of which Swedenborg elaborates in his theological works. There are heavenly landscapes—gardens Swedenborg experienced in the other world. And there are earthly landscapes—the gardens planted in time and space, reflecting human values, aspirations and change. In terms of inherent meanings, earthly gardens pose significant challenges to interpretation because they do not spring spontaneously from the gardener's thoughts and loves, as do heavenly gardens. Nor do they carry *specific* correspondence, as do gardens in the Word. Certainly every garden reflects the choices of the gardener, and gardens have been constructed to convey particular meanings and effects, as with the royal gardens of Louis XIV, intended to overwhelm the observer by the monarch's power, or the eighteenth-century landscape gardens of England, modelling classical values and structures of Italian Renaissance gardens. [23] But what of the meaning that flows from the nature of the plants themselves? There is of course a 'language of flowers', but different cultures assign different meanings, making significance seem arbitrary rather than intrinsic. Some meanings show up with uncanny regularity across cultures and time—red flowers for love; white ones for purity—hinting perhaps at a vestige of correspondence. Maybe our gardens have inherent meanings, but these meanings have become so muted that we can no longer discover the code. If the code is undiscoverable, might we then wonder what exactly we are seeking? When we manipulate nature for what we consider to be aesthetic or spiritual ends, are we grasping after some lost order? Or are we perhaps merely reiterating the condition of our fallen nature—forcing by an external, mediated route what used to flow spontaneously and directly from an internal one? Whatever gardens represent or signify, symbolize or mean, across centuries or cultures or worlds, they reflect human values and longings, especially for peace, beauty and order. And the more these values seem lost to the world at large, the more the garden becomes the sacred space for personal redemption and recovery.

Milton's garden epic

Two decades before Swedenborg's birth, John Milton, that great paradox of Puritan apologist and classical scholar, tackled this dilemma of fall and recovery in the greatest garden poem ever written, *Paradise Lost* (1667). The poem's fiercely pruned, and thus exotically blooming, language describes what Milton came to embrace as a 'fortunate' fall. The loss of Eden was tragic, occurring as it did in full knowledge and responsibility, but it was also 'fortunate' because it stimulated and elevated consciousness, thus making way for paradise regained. In Milton's view, the fallen Adam and Eve develop humility, reciprocity, and the shaping power of language, which is how I like to view human efforts at gardening in our world——a 'fortunate' fall from primordial innocence in Eden. Gardens illustrate our human efforts to impose order on the natural world, or perhaps to bring out its hidden wonder. We work with nature in order to transcend it, make one world point to another. Gardening can be seen as an effort to forge a language of growing things that whispers and murmurs, somewhere to the side of articulation, the untold realities behind and beyond this natural world. Just as the speech of angels falls 'into representations of gardens' in the other world, [24] so our efforts at gardening here on earth may represent a humble attempt to tune into celestial reverberation.

There are of course dangers in wielding correspondences, especially from pride of intelligence rather than from a love of truth and goodness. Swedenborg warns that people 'who [know] the science of correspondences, and want to use [their] own intelligence to explore the spiritual sense of the Word, can do violence to this Divine truth' because a knowledge of a few correspondences enables people 'to corrupt that sense, and even misapply it to proving false propositions'. [25] This degraded dynamic of seeking the spiritual sense exclusively through one's own limited understanding is anticipated by Milton's description of the dangerously eloquent snake in Eden. Embodying pride and misdirected eloquence, the snake tempts Eve through her vanity and sensuality, all in the guise of offering her the knowledge that will make her equal to God. By describing the tempter's movement towards Eve in terms of overblown and entrapping coils of rhetoric that float redundantly about the snake, Milton underscores the false reasoning that precipitates the expulsion from Eden. [26] As much as it might seem that we, like Milton's Eve, could master the spiritual sense through some revealed knowledge of correspondence, some appeal to our vanity or sense of self-sufficiency, in reality we cannot get at correspondences or the spiritual sense except through a relationship with God, and through a change of heart: 'Enlightenment comes only from the Lord', Swedenborg insists, 'and [only] to those who love truths because they are true, and make them their guide to a useful life. No others find enlightenment in the Word'. [27]

Though we have grown mostly deaf and blind to heaven's influx, and though we cannot think our way back into communion with heaven simply by knowing what some things signify, the sheer desire to see once more heaven's order in earthly landscapes and human communities, and to seek a place in that order, can serve good ends. Many readers of Milton's *Paradise Lost* have found the Adam and Eve who leave paradise, humbled but hand in hand, far more inspiring than the untested pair. Suffering and loss have awakened them to their limitations, their compassion for one another, and the value of the blessings they have forfeited and must now work to recover. Similarly, our humble labour to plant physical and spiritual gardens in the deserts we find in our lives can be a turn towards Eden and paradise regained.

I

Garden Correspondence

A ccording to Swedenborg, human life began on earth in a literal and figurative garden in close communion with heaven. When humans fell away from loving God above all, they left the garden, or rather they lost the heavenly state of effortless labour from love. Hard labour ensued. Now we struggle to build outside our hearts the gardens, or fruitful lives, that formerly grew spontaneously within our hearts. We till and weed and sweat, resisting the urge to take credit for the very effort that is itself a sign of our alienated state. Ironically, the act of weeding and watering these gardens so far removed from our first home is the only way back to something like a spiritual Eden. Likening the work of repentance to the work of weeding, Swedenborg asks, 'Can anyone work over a piece of ground thick with thorns, briars and nettles to make a garden until he has uprooted those weeds?' [1] When evil is removed by repentance, then we are 'grafted onto the Lord like a branch onto a vine'. [2] We must become gardeners in order to become gardens. At the same time, we need to acknowledge that we merely go through the motions, that it is God who tirelessly tends our gardens to bring forth fruit. Our cooperation and effort, however, are crucial, mirroring the three steps by which we allow ourselves to be saved. When we identify and weed out evils from our life (repentance), we can be grafted onto the Lord (reformation), and then good fruit begins to grow (regeneration). As we become wise and humble through this process, we spontaneously and gratefully return fruit to the Lord, at which point we are not only images but likenesses of God.

This harvest, or process, remakes us in the image and likeness of the Creator. The 'image' is the effort we make to counter our selfish and sensual belief that life is our own; the 'likeness' is the acknowledgment, freely given, that all life, including our own, is from God. [3] When we know and feel that our life is a gift, we internalize the paradise, or garden, from which we originally expelled ourselves. And we bear fruit once more.

The Book of Genesis, as explicated in Swedenborg's *Arcana Caelestia*, uses images of gardens and horticulture to lay out the process by which successive churches fell away from heaven, as well as the promise of recovery through individual regeneration. Swedenborg chose the image of a gardener tilling the soil, framed on either side with cornucopia, as the prefatory ornament to his *Arcana Caelestia* (Fig. 1 opposite).

Many of Swedenborg's other theological works also address the correspondence of gardens, though not as thoroughly or systematically as *Arcana Caelestia*. Swedenborg's ongoing interest in gardens

Fig. 1. Gardener tilling the soil. Frontispiece to Swedenborg's *Arcana Caelestia*.

is highlighted by the garden motif that appears on title pages of later works. *The Four Doctrines*, *Continuation on the Last Judgment*, *Divine Love and Wisdom*, *Divine Providence* and *Apocalypse Revealed* all bear a prominent ornament of a cherub watering a potted plant in a garden, accompanied by the words *cura et labore*, 'with care and work' (See Fig. 2 overleaf).

Swedenborg's engagement with horticulture can be seen in the garden he laid out at his home in Stockholm, in the ornaments he chose as frontispieces to his published works, in the way he tended and enjoyed his garden, and in the many garden references (more than 1,200) throughout his published theological writings. These references to gardens fall into three main areas: 1) the Garden of Eden in particular, representing a celestial or un-fallen state; 2) gardens in general, representing the intelligence or rational thought that provides the ground for the work of regeneration; and 3) gardens as images for the Word.

1. The garden in Eden

The garden in Eden differs from all later gardens. According to Swedenborg, it was not a specific spot in time and space but a pure state of heart and mind existing with the people of the most ancient church.[4] These early people did indeed live in beautiful external

Fig. 2. Cherub watering a garden. Frontispiece to some of Swedenborg's theological works published in Amsterdam.

gardens wherever they pitched their tents, not because the natural world was lovelier then than now, but because paradise was already within their hearts. The words in Genesis describing the location and orientation of this first garden describe as well the state of the earliest people: 'A garden in Eden, from the east' signifies the intelligence of celestial people, which flows in from the Lord through love.[5] The garden means intelligence; Eden, the celestial state; and 'from the east', facing the Lord in all things. These people knew things spontaneously from love. They certainly used their minds to think deep thoughts—they tended their gardens—but they attributed everything to the Lord and therefore felt no sense of labour or personal property: ' "tilling [the garden] and caring for it" means [. . .] to enjoy all these things but not to possess them as [one's] own, since they are the Lord's'. [6] Fourteen centuries before Swedenborg, Augustine of Hippo similarly describes this early pleasure in gardening: 'Man was placed in Paradise with the understanding that he would till the land not in servile labor but with a spiritual pleasure befitting his dignity'. And much like Swedenborg's descriptions of the highest angels, Augustine goes on to identify innocence and wisdom as properties of paradise within: 'What is more innocent than this work [gardening] for those who are at leisure, and what is more provocative of profound reflection for those who are wise?' [7] However, when people fell away from this early innocence and wisdom and began to relish bodily and earthly things instead of heaven, when they put themselves before God and rejected charity, then they were 'sent out of the garden of Eden to till the ground'. [8] The Fall, then, is not the fact of having to work, since there was always tilling in Eden, but the relocation outside Eden and dislocation from God. To be expelled from Eden means to lose all intelligence or understanding of truth, which a garden represents, and all love, wisdom or 'will for good', which Eden represents. [9] To till ground *outside* Eden is to kill Abel, or charity. Once outside Eden, people continue to tend the earth but now with sweat and labour in place of unselfconscious joy. The pain associated with labour (whether to produce crops or children) is misunderstood if it implies that work itself is a fallen condition. For Swedenborg the opposite is true. Work is salvation.

Gardens, and the effort to tend them, illustrate that heaven flowers through work and uses. The mythology of an effortless or passive paradise is no less than nightmarish for those who value the dignifying power of work. Robert Pogue Harrison's study of gardens and their mirroring of the 'human condition' explores this very idea of the care required by gardens, which makes them meaningful in human terms. [10] Heaven is not an escape nor a retreat but daily commitment to lives of fruitful service. Symbolically, we have to tend gardens one way or the other; the question is where and how. In Eden we tend them joyfully and effortlessly, with full awareness that we have little to do with the miracle of growth and fruition. Outside Eden, we labour hard and self-consciously, believing our effort and talent shape the harvest. Attributing good to ourselves, like hoarding manna, leaves us exhausted and our stores worm-ridden, whereas acknowledging that all good is from God brings peace and pleasure in the work itself: 'In ploughing and harvesting you shall rest'. [11] When we love work, we know rest.

Having lost paradise, we might ask, how do we re-establish ourselves in Eden, or at least lay out our gardens towards the east? We gain some insight by looking at what Swedenborg says the most ancient people did wrong, and by working with what we have. Genesis describes how to live off the produce of Eden through the command to eat of every tree except one. According to Swedenborg, this edict means that the most ancient people were permitted to take in knowledge from every source, in heaven and on earth, as long as they did not proceed in an inverted order, outside in, 'by reasoning about heavenly things from worldly knowledges, instead of thinking about worldly things from heavenly things'. [12] These early people fell, Swedenborg suggests, because the inverted order of their lives blocked influx from heaven. As inheritors of that fallen condition we can be redirected towards heaven through the process of being regenerated. We can use knowledge and reason ('right reason' as Milton described it, not to be confused with self-serving ratiocination) to allow our understandings to be raised into heaven, and from that light, see that our wills need to reside there also. When our love and actions, not just our thoughts, dwell in heaven, then we acquire wisdom. As regeneration progresses, love resumes its rightful first place, and understanding (the garden) flows once more through love (Eden) from the Lord (eastward). Eden therefore is not the exclusive domain of the most ancients. It represents the original innocence, or recovered purity, of any individual.

2. Gardens as intelligence and rational thought

The majority of references to gardens in the Word are not to Eden. By the second chapter of Genesis, the process of exile from Eden has already begun. The many subsequent references to gardens, for the most part, signify the possibility of regeneration, that is, the possibility of a recovered paradise *within* each individual. Specifically Swedenborg claims that gardens represent intelligence or rational thought, which is the means by which regeneration can be effected. A person's rational level is compared to a garden in the Word because in heaven a person's rational capacity actually appears as a garden when the Lord flows into it. [13] On earth, however, our minds are not as fertile for divine sowing as are the minds of angels. Our gardens take time and labour.

Regeneration, or the formation of a new will and a new understanding open to God, is likened repeatedly in Swedenborg's work to planting and gardening, as in the following passage from *Arcana Caelestia*:

> regeneration is like the activity of planting. When a tree is planted it grows into branches, leaves, and fruit, then from seeds in the fruit it grows into new trees, and so on. A person's regeneration is similar, which also explains why in the Word a person is compared to a tree, and one who has been regenerated to a garden or paradise. [14]

The physical world, like the Bible, is filled with images of rebirth and regeneration. In his *The True Christian Religion*, Swedenborg lists such images as 'the way all the earth's products flower in springtime'; 'the way any tree, shrub or flower grows from the first month of warm weather until the last'; 'early morning and late evening showers'; 'dew, which when it falls makes flowers open'; and perhaps most ephemeral, 'the [fragrances] from gardens and fields'. [15] These things do not simply reflect but actually contain spiritual essences: 'every detail of nature is as it were a tunic, sheath or clothing enclosing spiritual things'. [16]

Although we inhabitants of this earthly world have lost the ability to be affected spontaneously by correspondences we can at least learn *about* them, about concepts of regeneration and spiritual life, and then look to nature for illustration. Swedenborg claims that if we know anything about regeneration, or if we even 'want to know', we can see in any flower the threshold to heaven because just as blossoms precede fruit, so the desire to implant in life the good of intelligence and wisdom precedes the actual production of uses. [17] The mere desire to know spiritual things and to be useful can turn the smallest flower into a portal on eternity.

The most ancients knew from instinct, and the ancients from instruction, that the entire natural world was a stage for expressing the presence of the Divine. [18] During the first falling away from heaven, when the correspondences originally written *in* the natural world had to be linguistically recorded *as* a written text, the successive churches themselves became encoded as gardens. In *Arcana Caelestia*, Swedenborg writes that 'In the Word Churches are frequently described as "gardens"', and this comparing of churches to gardens has its 'origins in the representations in heaven, where also gardens of indescribable beauty are sometimes manifested in accordance with the spheres of faith. [...] This is quite clear from many places in the Word'. [19] The words on the page, however, are not living correspondences until they lead to engagement with realities beyond the page. Swedenborg protests that correspondences are not mere metaphors, by which I think he means humanly selected linguistic placeholders for something else. Citing a passage about the planting of cumin, wheat, barley and spelt (Isaiah 28.23-6), Swedenborg says: 'These things look like metaphors, but they are real correspondences, which serve to describe the reformation and regeneration of a member of the Church'.[20] Correspondences are an actual relationship between heaven and earth. There are gardens in both worlds, for instance, because the worlds are interdependent: 'all things on this planet, including those in its vegetable kingdom, correspond to spiritual realities that exist in heaven'.[21] Correspondences can be seen as living connections that reintegrate natural things into their larger spiritual context. Metaphor says one thing is like another; correspondence is the actual flowing of one thing into another. A telephone resting on a desk is a metaphor for the possibility of communication, whereas a conversation on that phone is correspondence. The phone is quickly forgotten in the life of the conversation, just as successful words disappear into the meanings they evoke, and just as gardens in heaven recede into the thoughts and feelings that produced them. As we become regenerated and more fully attuned to spiritual reality, perhaps the word 'garden' and gardens themselves (foliage and flowers, scents and colours) will evoke their heavenly counterparts, not just the heavenly gardens but the very thoughts, speech and love of angels that sustain those gardens. Then the worlds will be not just related but in conversation.

3. The Word as a garden

In *Doctrine of the Sacred Scripture*, Swedenborg describes the Word as being 'like a garden, a heavenly paradise, in which are delicacies and delights of every kind'. [22] The delicacies relate to fruits and the delights to flowers. In the middle of the garden that represents the Word there are 'trees of life, and near by, fountains of living water with forest trees round about the garden'. [23] The place of human beings in this garden, as well as their ability to sense and enjoy it, depends on the level or quality of each person's interaction with the Word: 'The [person] who is principled in Divine Truths from doctrine abides in the centre of the garden where are the trees of life, and is in the actual enjoyment of its delicacies and delights'. Those who are principled in truths, but only from the literal sense and not from deeper teachings, live 'in the outskirts of the garden, and [see] only the forest'. And those who are in falsity and have confirmed this falsity in their mind, dwell well beyond the farthest boundaries of the garden, 'not even in the forest, but in a sandy plain beyond it, where there is not even grass'. [24] So the Word is like a garden, and our relationship to it is like our place in the garden. The Word, however, is not merely a seedbed for similes. When we are in a receptive state, our interaction with the Word becomes the experience itself of fruit.

Aware of the potentially deadening process of laying out the idea of correspondence in cerebral bits and pieces, Swedenborg steps back at moments and shares with us the actual *experience* of correspondence, which is a garden experience:

In the Lord's Divine mercy I too have been allowed [...] to see the Word of the Lord in its beauty in the internal sense [...] not when individual expressions are being explained as to their internal sense, but when every single thing is presented in a single sequence of thought. This may be called seeing a heavenly paradise by means of an earthly one. [25]

Swedenborg here uses the experience of seeing a heavenly paradise or garden through an earthly one to describe the beauty and power of the Word as a medium of conjunction between heaven and earth. When we truly experience the internal sense of the Word, not just read the words, we too will see heaven from any earthly garden. Blake describes this revelatory moment as seeing divinity in a humble flower and holding 'Infinity in the palm of your hand'. [26] Tennyson too celebrates the divine instruction in the smallest bit of nature, rightly approached:

> I hold you here, root and all, in my hand,
> Little flower—but if I could understand
> What you are, root and all, and all in all,
> I should know what God and man is. [27]

These moments of glimpsing divinity in the smallest detail of the physical world, or in the pattern behind the strands of language in revelation, is communion with heaven.

Although a garden seems like a humble metaphor to represent something as potent and encompassing as the Word, garden imagery pervades written revelation in powerful ways. From well-watered Eden, to a promised land flowing with milk and honey, to a 'fountain of gardens' in the Song of Solomon (4.15), garden motifs saturate Hebrew scripture. Gardens and vineyards fill the stories of the New Testament as well, and Christ himself is variously associated with garden locations and with cycles of fecundity, such as the grain of wheat that falls into the ground and dies in order to bring forth more fruit (John 12.24). Christ is buried in a garden and, in his risen state, first appears as a gardener. Vigen Guroian, in *The Fragrance of God*, calls the risen Christ 'the Master Gardener' and us 'his apprentices as well as the subject of his heavenly husbandry'. [28] Drawing on Augustine, Guroian equates the cross in Calvary with the tree of life in Eden, and Christ with 'the once forbidden fruit of which we may now freely partake'. [29] The garden from which the first people were expelled is thus recreated in Christ, and paradise is regained through internalization of Christ's message.

Not only do gardens and garden imagery appear throughout the Old and New Testaments, but the written Word is described *as* a garden by Swedenborg, and he also sees the Word appearing inside gardens in the other world. At its deepest level, the Word is the Lord Himself, Swedenborg says, which might explain why so many of the gardens of heaven have guards and checkpoints. Even the angels need to pause on holy thresholds, as Mary in the garden of Gethsemane is cautioned not to touch the risen Lord, not to assume, perhaps, that she grasps His divine identity, even if He has recognized her and called her by her name. There is a garden within each of us that is a gateway to the Divine, if only we can remember that we are not God. The Lord is both the garden and the gardener, the voice walking in Eden, the burning bush that is not consumed, the God who knows our name. All ground is holy ground when it teaches us about our relationship to the Divine. Describing the carefully protected process of entering into the spiritual sense of the Word through correspondence, doctrine and enlightenment, Swedenborg says that 'the spiritual sense is not granted to anyone except by the Lord, and He guards it, just as the heaven of the angels is guarded, for this heaven possesses this sense'.[30] As stated earlier, enlightenment comes only from the Lord because the Word is from Him and He is in it.[31] Further, when we love truths because they are true and use them to live useful, flowering lives, then we too are in the Lord and the Lord is in us. The Word, the Lord, gardens and the regenerating soul are all seamlessly interwoven to produce a cloth called heaven. Little wonder, then, that Swedenborg, finding himself in these heavenly gardens, seems overwhelmed, at times speechless, in the presence of their beauty and significance.

II

Gardens in Heaven

G ardens in heaven are more beautiful and more interesting than any gardens on earth, and more beautiful and
interesting than Swedenborg's descriptions of them. This
section looks at Swedenborg's challenges with describing heavenly
gardens, his attention to gardens as teaching sites and metaphors,
and his description of six particular gardens in heaven, each of which
offers new ground for further speculation.

With regard to detailed descriptions of the countless gardens of
heaven, Swedenborg offers surprisingly little. Or rather, he offers
tantalizing testimony to what he will not describe. Although gardens
pervade heaven—'everywhere in the heavens gardens appear, producing leaves, flowers and fruits according to the states of the Church
with the angels'[1]—and although every plant has a specific use—'a
spiritual use in the spiritual world, and both a spiritual and a natural
use in the natural world'[2]— Swedenborg will not dwell on details or
give specific information about particular plants or gardens. He deals

rather in the most general of terms, as in the following passage from *Apocalypse Explained*:

> The spiritual use [of plants] is for the various states of the mind, and the natural use is for the various states of the body. It is well known that minds are refreshed, recreated, and stimulated, or on the other hand that drowsiness, sadness, or fainting is induced, by the odors and flavors of different kinds of plants; also that the body is healed by the various solutions, purgations, and remedies made from plants, and on the other hand, is destroyed by the poisons extracted from them.
>
> In the heavens the external spiritual use derived from them is the refreshment of minds, and the internal is the representation of Divine things in them, and thereby also the elevation of the mind. For the wiser angels see in them the quality of affections in a series. These, with what lies hidden in them, are manifested in the varieties of flowers in their order, also in the variegations of color and odor. For every ultimate affection which is called natural, although it is spiritual, derives its quality from an interior affection, which pertains to intelligence and wisdom, and these derive their quality from use and the love of it. In a word, from the soil in the heavens nothing but use blooms forth, for use is the plant soul. [3]

What a treasure of information we almost get. We are told *that* use blooms forth, but not what the blossoms look like, nor which flowers heal what deficiencies. It would seem that Swedenborg's descriptions do not intend to bring heaven to us, but rather us to heaven, where we can experience these gardens first-hand.

In place of the disappointment of not experiencing something more substantial and vivid from the eyewitness account of a person who spent more than a quarter of a century in heaven, we have the strange comfort of being forced back upon our own experience and imagination. The journey to heaven becomes both a homecoming and a venturing forth because heaven is the symbolic garden we have tended all along. Swedenborg likens our life to a tree that grows from seed to fruit, reproducing itself until there is an entire garden. 'And if [we] will believe it', he says, 'that same garden remains with [us] after death; [we] dwell in it, and [are] every day delighted with the sight of it, and with the enjoyment of its fruits'.[4] Our garden is immediately recognizable in the way it springs from the quality of our life and imagination, but it is indescribable because it is enhanced by divine hues, variety and radiance.

This tension between the familiar and the indescribable underpins many of the horticultural references in Swedenborg's work. At times heaven is as immanent as the scent of a velvet-petalled peony fallen sideways under its own weight. At other times it seems as distant and abstract as the halting language that collapses under the weight of the inexpressible. The hue of heavenly flowers is 'so resplendent that the colours of this world cannot compare with them',[5] and the process by which angels appear *as* gardens can be expressed only in defeated terms, 'this [process] is done in a celestial manner which no one except those in heaven can conceive, nor can it ever be expressed in words'.[6] Language fails, unable to convey spiritual reality. One world cannot be imported easily into another. The tension between matter and spirit, immanence and transcendence, or what can be expressed and contained versus what cannot, describes the human paradox of being born into matter but pointed towards spirit. Gardens embody this paradox. Tiny physical seeds buried in dirt, acted on by heat and light, grow into fruitful images of heaven and the Divine. Their sheer abundance exemplifies infinity; their ongoing fruitfulness symbolizes eternity.[7]

The symbolic and pedagogic power of gardens and of the various stages of cultivation is not lost on Swedenborg. To illustrate spiritual realities he draws on gardens throughout his theological work, most obviously as spiritual correspondences, but also as scientific illustrations, as literary metaphors and as physical settings for inspiration and instruction. By looking at these references to gardens (thinly described though they be) we can learn about heaven and ourselves, particularly how to get each back inside the other.

Gardens as teaching sites

When Swedenborg describes newcomers arriving in the other world and their fantasies (turned nightmares) about heaven as a pleasure garden without work of any sort,[8] we see dramatized the mistaken notion that we can inhabit heaven through its external effect (gardens) rather than its internal cause (useful life). After a few days of repetitive sensual stimulation void of useful work, these newcomers run frantically about the garden trying to find an exit. They are trapped in their own conception of heaven as a physical return to Eden and to sensual pleasure. The angels release these desperate newcomers once they have taken the lesson to heart, that is, when they have fully experienced the suffocating reality of their exclusively sensual conception.

But gardens are also used in more subtle ways in heaven to lead newcomers from the familiar to the unfamiliar, from the best they could formerly imagine to a gradual acceptance of heaven as something that lies *beyond* their furthest understanding and experience of earthly delight. In this way, gardens become gateways to the initially unimaginable. For example, *Arcana Caelestia* describes the process by which newcomers begin to grasp heavenly life through exposure to gardens:

> Almost everybody entering the next life is ignorant of what heavenly blessedness and happiness are [...] Therefore so that upright persons who do not know what heavenly joy is may come to know and recognize it they are taken first of all to the gardens there, which surpass anyone's entire imagination. [...] These persons now suppose that they have entered the heavenly paradise, but they are taught that even this is not true heavenly happiness, and so they are then given to know about the inward states of joy that enter their inmost being. After this they are brought into a state of peace that reaches to their inmost being, at which point

they declare that no part of such experience could possibly be expressed in words or even conceived of. [9]

Gardens in heaven thus serve as sites for gentle and aesthetic orientation to a new life, as newcomers gradually fathom a reality that exceeds former conceptions and touchstones. The orientation process is both external and internal. The gardens display unimaginable external beauty 'surpass[ing] anyone's entire imagination', and they reach internally as well, inspiring inexpressible and inconceivable peace at the level of 'inmost being'.

Heavenly gardens disillusion newcomers about former fantasies that heaven has anything to do with inactivity and mere sensual pleasure. They also help newcomers begin to conceive of levels of external beauty and internal peace that were previously inconceivable. But gardens also serve a third purpose as vehicles of *ongoing* instruction, namely, to reveal inner states of angels. When angels see changes in their gardens they 'examine and investigate in themselves' so that they can then 'perform the work of repentance'. [10] In addition to supporting self-examination on an individual level, gardens foster communal reflection and growth, as when the angels explain to Swedenborg how heaven's landscapes reflect the relationship between faith and charity, and how changes in this relationship are mirrored in the surroundings. Where faith and charity are separated, 'not so much as grass grows; and any patch of greenery is produced by thorns and briars'; where faith and charity are joined, however, 'there are parkland gardens, flower-gardens and shrubberies, the more beautiful, the more closely they [faith and charity] are combined'. [11] Gardens in heaven provide instruction in at least four ways: they expose misperceptions that sensual pleasure is an end in itself; they press consciousness and imagination beyond earthbound limitations; they facilitate self-examination and repentance for individual angels; and they provide a spiritual barometer of the balance between faith and charity. But what do these gardens, these versatile tools, look like?

It would seem that one of the greatest challenges Swedenborg faces in describing heavenly gardens is to make them hold still, and to find the right words. Even more than earthly gardens' continual fluctuation from day to day and season to season, heavenly gardens fluctuate with states of mind and heart, in accord with angels' reception of the Divine:

> the heavens in which [the angels] are, and which appear to the sight altogether like our lands, but full of paradises, flower beds, and shrubberies, are not permanent like the lands on our globe, but come into existence in a moment in the exact measure of the reception of the Divine truth by the angels [...]. [12]

Because we are unfamiliar with such heavenly phenomena, having only 'a natural idea, which is according to what [we] see', [13] we can scarcely imagine the vitality of heavenly gardens. Plants and flowers move and change, sometimes turning into other species of plants, or even animals. [14] In heaven, a river of correspondence flows between inner and outer realities, between angels' reception of God and the foliage at their feet. Given our earthly dependence on time and space, on cycles of natural growth, and on distinct categories of minerals, plants and animals, it can be unsettling to try to imagine the flux of heaven's gardens. Certainly the effort to picture these gardens requires some altered state of consciousness. Once when Swedenborg is describing the gardens of the natural angels, he stops short, as if suddenly aware of harm——'but these things are not to be written in this way for the world lest they [spirits] seek heavenly things in phantasies'. [15] Does Swedenborg see something destructive or distorting to the earthly mind in its being given, second-hand, too much external detail without the actual experience of spiritual life? Is he perhaps resisting offering his own view, knowing that each of us will see a unique spiritual reality? Swedenborg can tell us only what he sees, which changes continually before his eyes, and he relies upon earthly language, which cannot fully encompass spiritual phenomena.

Although Swedenborg frequently claims that the natural and spiritual worlds closely resemble each other, so much so that 'they cannot be distinguished. I have seen them, and could see no difference', [16] he repeatedly testifies to the indescribable or incommunicable nature of that other world, especially its gardens: 'few of these things can be described; those that cannot be described are innumerable, for as they are in their origin spiritual they do not fall into the ideas of the natural [person], and consequently not into the expressions of [his or her] language'. [17] Not to leave us in despair, however, Swedenborg adds an exception. Spiritual concepts and spiritual reality find a ready vessel in the regenerating mind:

24

'when wisdom builds for itself a habitation, and makes it comfortable to itself, everything that lies inmostly concealed in any science or in any art flows together and accomplishes the purpose'. [18] If we cannot experience heavenly gardens now, we will someday. Swedenborg will not so much transcribe the details of the beautiful gardens he experienced there as tell us how to live here and now so that when we get there, one day, we ourselves will be gardens worth inhabiting. The gardens of heaven are thus not a destination but a manifestation, and the lives we live on earth are the seeds being planted.

Swedenborg's attempts to share his experience of heavenly gardens with an audience that might not be able to understand him resembles the character Janie in Zora Hurston's novel *Their Eyes Were Watching God* (1937). Few comparisons seem as unlikely as that between Swedenborg and Hurston's narrator Janie, but the substance of their stories is powerfully similar. Janie travels in a number of worlds. She has been 'tuh de horizon and back', returning with wisdom to share. After her adventure of loving others and learning things about herself—and ultimately losing things in a way that teaches her how to truly value them—Janie returns home with seeds in her breast pocket, warmed by a heart that in being broken has learned how to love. She is an image of paradise regained or Eden internalized, and the story she tells is about God's love and the different shape it takes in every human breast: 'Love is lak de sea. It's uh movin' thing, but still and all, it takes its shape from de shore it meets, and it's different with every shore'. [19] The narrator's voice bears witness to the universal draw of divine love, but in a tone exquisitely coloured by dialect and class. Hurston's narrative creates the speaking presence of a voice that pervasively and paradoxically points out the inferiority of talking to the experience of living: 'you got tuh go there tuh know there [...] nobody else can't tell yuh and show yuh'. In the end Janie's message, told in an emotional, uneducated, sensual voice that couldn't be more different than Swedenborg's, boils down to surprisingly familiar wisdom. There are two things everyone has to do: '[t]hey got tuh go tuh God, and they got tuh find out about livin' fuh theyselves'.[20] This statement underscores Swedenborg's explanation of what it means to be human, or to be an 'image and likeness' of the Creator. Although we experience life as our own and thus act freely and independently (a condition Swedenborg describes as being an *image* of God), we need also to acknowledge that our life is not in fact our own but God's (a condition Swedenborg describes as being a *likeness* of God).[21] We are responsible to both realities—independence and humility—and only by inhabiting both will we return with seeds pressed against our hearts, becoming ourselves the gardens we hope to find in heaven.

The gardens Swedenborg describes in the other world are well ordered and fruitful. They embody the grounding in good from which truth springs: 'Truths increase immensely when they proceed from good [...] This increase is like the production of fruit from a tree, and multiplication from seeds, from which arise whole gardens'.[22] Swedenborg writes that people who love truth and do good live in gardens in the other world:

those who have loved branches of knowledge and used them to further their power of reason, and thereby gained understanding for themselves, and at the same time have acknowledged God [...] live in gardens, where they see flower beds and lawns beautifully laid out, with rows of trees round about, with openings leading to walkways. The trees and flowers change every day. [23]

Not only do angels live in beautiful gardens that express their loves, but their interactions with the gardens refine their understanding and enrich their delight: 'Everything they see brings a general feeling of pleasure to their minds, and constantly the variations bring them new pleasure in particular details'. And because everything in heaven 'correspond[s] to divine attributes, and [angels] have knowledge of correspondences', angels are constantly filled with new knowledge, which in turn perfects their spiritual rational faculty. [24] Heavenly gardens both reflect and elevate the consciousness of those who dwell in them, like spirals opening towards God. The spiral moves upward as beautiful lives create garden surroundings. These gardens in turn teach lessons to further edify and uplift, generating yet more lovely gardens. The endless progression dizzies the earthly mind.

All three heavens (celestial, spiritual and natural) have gardens according to the angels' reception of the light and heat of the spiritual sun. [25] The gardens of each heaven are distinguished by the fruit produced. The fruit of inmost or celestial gardens produces oil; the fruit of spiritual or intermediate gardens produces wine; and the fruits of the first or outermost heaven produce both oil and wine, but to a lesser degree than the other two heavens. [26] Complicating this view of the produce of the gardens in each of the three heavens is the teaching that whereas the innermost heaven receives the Lord's light 'as good which is called charity', and the middle heaven receives light 'as truth which is rooted in charity', the outermost heaven receives it 'as a paradise garden'. [27] Does this mean that only the outermost heaven manifests gardens? Swedenborg sees gardens in all three heavens. He talks about them and has experiences in them. The singling out of one heaven as the only one that receives the Lord's light as gardens suggests, perhaps, that the gardens of the middle and inmost heaven remain unnoticed by the inhabitants themselves, unless their attention is drawn to their surroundings, as when Swedenborg visits and asks questions. These angels are so absorbed in doing and living that they notice their gardens as little, perhaps, as we notice oxygen when we are happily absorbed in a mental or physical task.

In addition to describing the general order and fruit of heavenly gardens, Swedenborg describes some specific gardens where, not surprisingly, he learns particular things about heavenly life. Amongst the gardens he visits are the following six: 1) the garden around the Temple of Wisdom; 2) Andramandoni; 3) the garden state of a long-married couple; 4) rose gardens; 5) a wedding garden; and 6) a spiral of trees. A close reading of each of these gardens fills in some speculative detail about spiritual reality.

1. The garden around the Temple of Wisdom

What is perhaps most striking about Swedenborg's description of the garden surrounding the Temple of Wisdom, in *Conjugial Love*, [28] is the lack of description, as if the temple must not be outdone by the garden surrounding it. In the company of two angels, Swedenborg follows an ever-brightening light, ascending a steep path to the top of a hill in the southern zone of heaven. He finds a 'magnificent' gate, which a porter opens upon seeing the angel companions. An avenue of palm trees and laurels curves around until it reaches a garden. Unlike the geometric paths of Renaissance gardens, or even Swedenborg's own grid-like layout for his garden (see Fig. 3, p. 86), this curving avenue suggests a mediated balance between natural lines and human design. Once inside the garden, Swedenborg sees at its centre the Temple of Wisdom, much like the tree of life and the tree of knowledge at the centre of Eden. As if to reinforce that the fruit of this garden is wisdom, replicas of the temple appear throughout the garden. The image of one temple generating others resembles the description, in Swedenborg's *The True Christian Religion*, of the potentially limitless expansion of a person's intelligence and wisdom: 'each of which is capable of growth as a tree grows from seed, and woods and gardens from trees, for here there is no limit'. The passage goes on to describe in organic terms the relationship of intelligence and wisdom to memory, understanding and will. The human memory is the soil in which intelligence and wisdom are planted; the understanding is the medium in which they germinate; and the will is the medium in which they bear fruit. [29] Appropriately, at the Temple of Wisdom, this most spiritual of sites, fecundity is represented not by foliage and flowers but by replicated temples—a garden of temples. Into one of these offshoot temples Swedenborg gains entrance: 'We went up to one, and on the door-step spoke with our host, explaining why we had come and how we had arrived there'.[30] *How* he made the journey seems to be part of the qualification for entry. Beginning with desire (passion or affection) to see the temple, he asks angels the way, then in their company he follows the light up a steep path, passes through a gate, and walks a curved avenue. This journey reflects one way to approach heaven. Begin with desire; follow the light; keep good spiritual company; expect steep ways and barriers; and trust that the curve is sometimes the most direct route.

2. Andramandoni

Andramandoni, the garden Swedenborg describes in *Conjugial Love* as representing the delights of heavenly marriage love, provides a fascinating text when juxtaposed to the garden surrounding the Temple of Wisdom. Both gardens share some elements: palm trees and laurels lining curved ways, a locked gate, and an angel guard. In Andramandoni, however, the curved way extends into a spiral, and the gate leads to a bridge and then another gate before reaching the garden itself. These details (spiral, bridge, and second gate) suggest a place or state that, even more than the Temple of Wisdom, is additionally protected and deeply embedded:

> I went in and saw olive-trees, with vines running between the trees and hanging down. Beneath and between the trees there

were flowering shrubs. In the middle was a grassy circle, in which husbands and wives and young men and women were sitting in pairs. At the centre of the circle there was a rise in the ground with a fountain leaping into the air due to the force of the water. When I came close by, I saw two angels dressed in purple and red engaged in conversation with those who were sitting on the grass; they were talking about the source of conjugial love and its delights. Since this love was the subject, they were listened to eagerly and given full attention, and they were uplifted as if by the fire of love in what the angels said. [31]

Instead of a temple, a grassy circle occupies the centre, with couples seated all around, and at the heart, a leaping fountain. Two angels in purple and red (a married couple perhaps) converse with the other couples, instructing them about the nature of use. We learn that to be useful is to be active. '[L]ove and wisdom without use are merely abstract ways of thinking', they say, 'which also after a brief stay in the mind, pass away like winds'. But when love and wisdom are joined in use, they become 'reality'. [32] This beautiful and sequestered garden with its focus on water and love recalls ancient eastern gardens, which were characteristically built around a central source of moving water, while the emphasis on rhetorical activity resembles a Greek setting and the Socratic pursuit of truth, gardens in Ancient Greece often being venues for education and philosophical debate. The style of communication underscores the insistence on active engagement.

The angels encourage question and answer, not lecture format, 'for if something is merely heard it may be perceived at the time, but the impression does not last, unless the hearer also thinks about it for himself and asks questions'. [33] Like the temple at the centre of the previous garden, the fountain of water at the centre of Andramandoni presents another image of truth. The leaping water underscores vitality and activity, and perhaps accommodation. When Swedenborg visits the rose garden we will again see water at its centre, but this time the angels drink from the fountain.

The emphasis on use and activity in Andramandoni is heightened by the focus on couples and love. From Andramandoni Swedenborg learns about love, especially about its origin and expression. Like the fountain 'leaping into the air due to the force of the water', love surges from a divine source and expresses that source by flowing into use. The conclusion the angels give, which Swedenborg conveys to us, is that 'fruitfulness, propagation and reproduction are the means of continuing creation; and the only possible source of creation is out of Divine love through Divine wisdom in Divine use'. [34] Propagation and reproduction in heaven have to do with useful deeds and ideas, or spiritual offspring. The scene reinforces the lesson about balance and reciprocity between love and wisdom, both between partners and within individuals. We do not hear any details about the plants or fruit of this garden, but surely the sweetest fruits are the couples themselves, seated about the fountain, and the conversations that flow from them. If we were there with Swedenborg we could enjoy both the sense and sound of these voices. Grateful as we are for the ideas, we miss the first-hand experience of the tone of celestial voices, which is a perfect balance of love and wisdom, like the sound of running water. [35] It would take a poet to bring back the burble, and a gardener to bring back the gardens. Ironically, Swedenborg was both a poet and a gardener, as well as a musician, but for reasons we may never fully welcome, he mostly left those selves behind when travelling on spiritual business. Additionally, Swedenborg seems to be the only uncoupled element in the scene, perhaps because his role is to remain disengaged enough to observe and record and communicate to other realms. One of Swedenborg's great gifts is his ability to function in celestial, spiritual and natural modes. He is celestial enough to experience life amongst the highest angels, spiritual enough to reflect and ponder what it all means, and natural enough to drag the concepts down to us, urging them into language and matter, for our sakes.

3. The garden state of a long-married couple

The scene of partners *in* the Andramandoni garden is nicely matched by another scene in *Conjugial Love* in which married lovers *wear* a garden.

Swedenborg, meditating on marriage love, witnesses two naked children (*infantes*) [36] at a distance. When they come nearer, they appear dressed in flowers, 'small wreaths of flowers adorned their heads, and decorative bands of lilies and roses of blue colour hung obliquely across their chests from shoulders to hips'. [37] A woven garland of leaves and olives binds them together. When they come closer they appear in the 'prime of life', clothed now in garments that carry garden imagery woven into the fabric itself: 'gowns and tunics of shining silk with a pattern of the loveliest flowers you could see woven into it'. [38] Once beside Swedenborg, they breathe on him a sweet odour 'like that of fresh vegetation in gardens or fields' and then engage him with the question 'What have you seen?' They seem to accommodate their instruction to his response, as if they can teach only to a receptive state: 'Since you told us [. . .] that as we approached a breath of spring-like warmth spread over you with pleasant scents as from a garden, we shall explain why this was'. [39] The instruction, much like that in Andramandoni, addresses the concept of useful life as the seat of love. Husband and wife temper each other, and this tempering or mutual support 'happens as the result of and in proportion to the services which each [wife and husband] performs for the mutual help of their community'. [40] Love flows outward to serve others, and flows the more freely as partners balance each other. Delights follow according to the use, which is according to the balance in the marriage. Where reciprocity is most careful and perfect, 'where heat is evenly combined with light', the highest uses flow. The most perfect balance of all, of course, is where heat and light are so perfectly balanced that they make one entity, in the Lord, the wellspring for all gardens and heavenly marriages.

In this powerful scene with the flower-decked couple not only does Swedenborg gain first-hand confirmation about the interdependence of love and use in marriage, but we see a procession of images or symbols suggesting a number of additional readings. Most obviously there is the movement from infancy to adulthood, a microcosm of the heavenly lifespan, culminating in an ageless present tense. There is also the movement from nakedness to flower-clothing to garments woven with floral designs. This change from nakedness to a clothed state reflects less the 'loss' of Eden than the development of art and representation. Pictures of flowers replace the flowers themselves. The changing appearance of the couple might also embody for us the movement of meaning and experience outward through the three heavens, from pure innocence, to adorning flowers, to pictures of flowers, until we get to the furthest remove of our own consciousness and the translated words taking shape before us. The concepts come through, but bearing traces of the unthinkably long distance they have travelled. Above all, we see a tableau of the paradox of solidity and transformation in spiritual reality. The scene might be taken for a postmodern film with bodies morphing, flowers turning into textiles, and perspectives shifting as the distance narrows between object and observer. Amidst all this change, however, comes the startling realization that this is Swedenborg's experience of the angels, not their own. Their experience is quite different: 'they gave a pleasant laugh, and said that while they were on their way they did not seem to themselves as children, or naked, or garlanded, but continually like they were then'. [41] In fact they have been this way 'for centuries'. Their ability to experience stability from within while providing a fluid text from without raises thoughts about the alignment between Swedenborg's view of angels' surroundings and the angels' own experience of living in those gardens. Whether or not this particular angel couple is conscious of a garden around them, or on them, they cannot help but breathe out, with every well-tempered contraction and expansion of their hearts and lungs, the garden within them. However we find meaning in individual plants or garden designs, we can perhaps take our earthly gardens for the breath of heaven, and hope for inspiration to become angels ourselves.

4. Rose gardens

Two companion scenes, taking place in heavenly rose gardens, create a profound sense of the interdependence between natural and spiritual worlds.

Once when Swedenborg is looking out a window towards the east, he sees seven women sitting in a rose garden drinking water from a spring. 'I gazed very hard to see what they were doing', he relates in *Conjugial Love*, 'and the intensity of my gaze made itself felt by them. So one of them nodded to me as an invitation. I left home and hurried to join them'.[42] Swedenborg's writing desk in his summer house in Stockholm faced a window overlooking his garden, where he could see rose beds. We might presume that this was the window through which he gazed, and that his own garden was another window through which he logged on to heavenly gardens and saw, as described earlier, 'a heavenly paradise by means of an earthly one'.[43] Upon first arriving at the rose garden of the seven angel wives, Swedenborg asks them where they come from. It seems odd for this new arrival from another world to ask these women where *they* come from. They do not respond directly, or rather they answer in a manner that highlights heavenly reality—identity being what one does. To the question of where they come from they answer who they are in terms of what they are doing: 'We are wives [...] engaged in a conversation about the delights of conjugial love'. [44] From the first contact they set the tone, and they maintain their influence throughout the exchange. Although the topic of marriage love seems characteristically feminine, the women's mode of response is interestingly distant, almost scientific: 'Many proofs have led us to conclude that these delights are those of wisdom'. [45] The words may of course be Swedenborg's rendition of what they say. They may not have used words at all. But the effect of their response is striking. Their reply so pleases Swedenborg's mind that he is lifted 'in the spirit' and made 'capable of more inward and clearer perception than ever before'. [46] This is a remarkable instance of Swedenborg recording how his mind is tempered and inspired by women's thoughts. He humbly asks permission to ask them questions so that he can learn more from them. One of the things he learns—'Every act of [conjunction] by means of love [...] involves acting, receiving and reacting'—positions wives in an active role and husbands in receptive roles. 'The delightful state of our love is the acting', the women say, '[t]he state of our husbands' wisdom is the receiving [...] and this too is the reacting [...] in proportion to what is felt'. [47] This dynamic also describes Swedenborg's own receptive and reactive role in his interaction with the wives. This is not to say that gender roles are fixed, or that this memorable relation tells us how all husbands and wives ought to interact. If that were the case, there would be nothing but rose gardens in heaven. But it is refreshing to watch Swedenborg learn from women and to glimpse celestial interaction between husbands and wives. Scenes like the rose garden show another face of heavenly marriage. These experiences describe and illustrate rather than prescribe, each one a splash of colour in a larger garden.

Several days after this conversation with the wives, Swedenborg again gazes through his window at the same women, but located in another rose garden. This time we see the garden itself:

> It was a magnificent rose-garden, the like of which I had never seen before. It was circular, and the roses were arranged to make a kind of rainbow. The outermost ring was made of roses with purple flowers, the next inner ring of flowers of a golden yellow, the one within this of blue, the inmost of light or shining green. Inside this rainbow of roses was a small pool of limpid water. [48]

The women again summon him from his position at the window. This time *they* ask the question that launches the conversation—has Swedenborg ever seen such beauty on earth? When he admits, 'Never', they make a string of statements that seems initially simple:

> Such things [as the garden] [...] are created by the Lord in a moment, and they represent something new on earth, since everything created by the Lord represents something. But see

if you can guess what this represents. Our guess is that it is the delights of conjugial love. [49]

This exquisite and unparalleled garden springs effortlessly and instantaneously from God. We know that everything created represents something else, and that this garden in particular represents something new on earth. But here some questions arise. What does this garden, unlike anything on earth, represent on earth? The angel wives suggest it represents conjugial love, but in what sense are the delights of conjugial love a new thing on earth? Swedenborg writes this book precisely because conjugial love is scarcely known on earth, in danger, in fact, of being lost altogether. [50] Or maybe what is new is this very book about conjugial love. The conversation seems to be part of the research for the book. The exchange is one of those wonderful moments when text and experience become fruitfully entangled. The author writes about the process of getting the material for his book on marriage. In this second rose garden scene we see evidence of his having checked his spiritual sources (what he learned from the women in the first rose garden) against earthly authority. Women on earth tell him he must be jesting if he believes the angel wives. Swedenborg carries the earthly response back to the angels: 'I remember this from what they said, so that I could report it to you, seeing that they find repugnant and in fact totally contradict what you told me by the spring, when I so eagerly drank it in and believed it'. [51] Not surprised by the earthly response, the angel wives explain that women will conceal these things from their purely natural husbands. The information is not contradictory; Swedenborg simply does not know how to read women's responses. If earthly women are masking the truth because of the unhealthy state of their marriages, or marriages in general, we get an inkling of what kind of reception Swedenborg might expect for this work in progress.

When the rose garden wives finish instructing Swedenborg, their husbands appear bearing good and bad grapes to illustrate the ideas expressed by their wives. The scene concludes with a young boy (who appeared earlier) returning with a written text that he holds out for Swedenborg to read aloud. The written passage exhorts the audience to 'know that' the delights of conjugial love ascend to the highest heaven, attaching to the delights of all heavenly loves, and to 'also know that' the pleasures of scortatory love descend to the lowest hell, attaching in similar fashion to the worst things there. Love carries us to the highest and the lowest levels. Through the two rose garden scenes Swedenborg learns privileged information from the mouths of angel wives. He learns of earthly sabotage and resistance to such secrets. He experiences the heavenly wives' utter competence in discourse and their husbands' supportive roles in confirming and illustrating what they say. The fruit the husbands bring turns the women's words back to garden display where the scene began, in rainbows of roses. Notably, the husbands introduce bad fruit into the garden, for a lesson, true, but it seems likely that angel wives with their protective instincts for the sphere of marriage love would hesitate to import bad fruit, even for instructive purposes. Finally, the element of the boy with the written text for Swedenborg to read (and later record) removes the issue of authority from any contest about gender (wives versus husbands) or hierarchy (age versus youth; heavenly wives versus earthly wives). Divine truth comes finally on a written page to be read and lived in both worlds. A written medium of conjunction. Swedenborg looks up from his writing to gaze at a rose garden and ends by reading aloud in heaven a passage that we read simultaneously in our minds. The rose garden scenes beautifully collapse writers, readers, speakers, and texts across the threshold of two worlds and times.

5. A wedding garden

Once when Swedenborg is walking with his 'feelings at rest' and his mind 'at peace', as he reports in his *Conjugial Love*, he sees a park and an avenue leading to a small palace. He goes there in spirit and asks the doorkeeper for admittance, which is granted since the pleasure of conjugial love shines from Swedenborg's eyes and irradiates his face. The garden of a newly married couple lies within. Swedenborg follows an avenue 'made of fruit-trees with their branches interlacing, so as to make a continuous wall of trees on either side' and enters a small garden 'fragrant with shrubs and flowers', all of which are arranged in pairs. [52] We hear that there are many such gardens around houses where weddings have taken place, but no further details. After seeing a picture of conjugial love on the faces of the couple and learning of its 'living force' from their conversation, Swedenborg offers his congratulations to the couple and goes out into the garden. Ironically but predictably, the garden as a sensual experience recedes even further when Swedenborg enters it. He sees a group of men 'on the right' and notices that everyone leaving the house rushes over to this group because the topic of conversation, marriage love, has 'some hidden power to attract the minds of them all'. Swedenborg listens to a wise man speaking on this subject and learns that the Lord's divine providence regarding marriage is in the smallest and the most universal things. There is conjunction not only between partners but within each partner through a marriage of the will and the understanding, 'the two of which act together on the smallest details of both mind and body'. [53] The wise man's explanation goes on at length, laying out the balance between and within organs in the body, all composing one system, as two married partners compose 'one fully human life'. Then lightning strikes. And strikes again. First as a signal to add something, then as confirmation. The colour, quality and position of the lightning, along with the sound and timing of the thunder, all contribute to the power of the non-verbal dimension of the conversation in the garden.

When the lightning first strikes—red on the right, and white on the left—Swedenborg describes it as 'gentle', but it is also invasive in that it 'penetrated the eyes to reach our minds and also enlighten them'. This is not a mere metaphor for insight but a substantive influx that influences the eye and the understanding. This is correspondence. Then comes thunder, 'a gentle murmur flowing down from the heaven of the angels and growing in volume'. After 'hearing and seeing this', the speaker says these phenomena are a 'sign and a warning' to add something further. [54] The lightning is a visible sign to the understanding, and the thunder is warning to the heart, a double appeal illustrating the very pairings discussed earlier. What needs to be added, the wise man says, is that the right signifies good and relates to the will, and the left signifies truth and relates to the understanding. Although this pairing seems even-handed, the illustrations that follow emphasize the priority of the right side, or the good of charity and the good of life. When the wise man finishes speaking two flashes of lightning appear again, milder than before, but this time depicting how the quality of the light on the left depends on the light on the right: 'the left-hand flash having its whiteness tinged with the ruddy fire of the right-hand one'. [55] These final flashes confirm that 'the whiteness of light [. . .] is the same as the radiance of fire'. Everyone then leaves, joyfully 'fired' by the lightning and the discourse concerning it.

This scene of instruction in the wedding garden is striking for its unaccountable aspects and heavenly resistance to verbal abstraction. We know that initially Swedenborg saw an image of conjugial love on the faces of the married couple, and that he learned of it as well from their conversation. But this is not the conversation we hear about, nor does he try to describe their faces. Rather, Swedenborg goes out into the garden where men are talking, and he listens to a wise man articulate the tenets of conjugial love. We get a second-hand experience, much like the instruction in the subsidiary temple in the garden outside the Temple of Wisdom. The information is accurate but needs supplementation from lightning and thunder, almost as if the talking in the garden 'about' love is a pale version of the experience of love radiating from the couple in the house. Talking about something is always a step removed from the lived experience, but a crucial step. The conversation in the garden that 'had some hidden power to attract the minds of them all' reminds us of the life of the understanding and the importance of struggling to find shape for ideas so that we can handle them, pass them back and forth, and try to apply them. The thunder and the lightning, however, remind us to watch and listen for the divine editing that turns words back into life, and understanding back towards humility. The thunder rolling outward from the inmost heaven tells of origins, the depths of which silence us with wonder. Finally, the dance of light and fire is not some equation we thought up but divine solar reality coming to us in mercifully mild forms to remind us of values that exceed our calculations.

6. A spiral of trees

In *The True Christian Religion*, Swedenborg describes how he and a group of visitors to a heavenly community are once escorted by a member of that community to a prince's garden. The angel guide tells them that in comparison even to heavenly gardens, this one is particularly magnificent. At first the visitors are disappointed, seeing only a single tree. The guide responds that this is the tree of life, and if their eyes are opened they will see the garden. They then indeed see a magnificent garden of trees arranged around the tree of life in the middle:

> These trees were planted in an unbroken row, extending outward and running in constant circles or rings, like a never-ending spiral. It was a perfect spiral of trees, in which one species followed another arranged in order of the nobility of their fruits. There was

a considerable gap between the beginning of the spiral and the tree in the middle, and this gap sparkled with gleams of light, which made the trees of the ring shine with a splendour running in graduated steps from the first to the last. The first trees were the most outstanding of all, luxuriant with the finest fruits; these were called trees of paradise, something never seen before because they do not, nor can they, exist on earth in the natural world. These were followed by trees that yield oil, and these by trees that yield wine. After these came trees with a fragrant scent, and finally trees with wood useful for making things. Here and there in this spiral or ring of trees were seats shaped out of tree-shoots brought and woven together from behind, enriched and embellished with their fruits. There were gates in this unbroken circle of trees, leading to flower gardens, and these leading to lawns, divided by plots and beds. [56]

This most detailed description comes, ironically, through the consciousness of spirits who could not at first see anything. Their response, however, is touchingly enthusiastic: 'Here is heaven made visible! Whichever way we turn our gaze, there is an impression made on us of heavenly paradise, beyond description'. [57] To see this garden, we learn, one must love to be useful for its own sake, not for glory, all of which nicely illustrates the leadership of this particular prince. He loves to serve rather than dominate; the beautiful garden is an effect, not a display, of his authority.

Amongst the many wonderful details in this tree garden, several stand out as richly paradoxical. This single garden produces the fruit earlier attributed to the gardens of all three heavens (oil, wine and wood), and the emphasis on continuity in the layout of the garden (unbroken rows, constant rings, never ending spiral and unbroken circles) is counterbalanced by markers and boundaries that separate one thing from another (gaps, gates and divisions). In terms of the single garden procuring all levels of fruit, we can imagine that any piece of heaven, rightly seen, is a microcosm of the whole. [58] As for the intermingling of repeated elements of continuity and division, it seems that in heaven hierarchy creates connection. The 'considerable gap' between the outer trees and the tree in the middle is the very space or separation that enlivens the periphery: 'The gap sparkled with gleams of light, which made the trees of the ring shine with a splendour'. Just as these trees of paradise cannot be described since they 'do not, nor can they exist on earth', so heavenly government, which vitalizes rather than oppresses, cannot be replicated on earth. Although we may not be able to reproduce spiritual order and spiritual gardens, we can be inspired by the thought of them and, ironically, by the gap that separates us from heaven.

The scene in this garden ends with instruction about the 'representation and meaning of each detail in that garden'. [59] The visitors find out, but we do not. This lack of information can be frustrating but curiously reassuring at the same time. We have a sense that learning in that wonderful garden has a life of its own and extends well beyond the text that draws our attention to it. We can speculate about significance, but in the end, we will have to go there to know there. As Swedenborg so often assures us, words alone cannot convey the reality of the other world.

III

Gardens in History

T his section traces six historical stages of gardening, from the ancient Middle East, to Greece and Rome, Islam, the Middle Ages, the Renaissance and finally, Swedenborg's own era——the eighteenth century. The overview is neither learned nor exhaustive. But in the light of Swedenborg's explanations of garden correspondence and his descriptions of gardens in heaven, it serves to provide some ground for speculating about the symbolic value of gardens through the ages. In taking a long historical view, I am interested in what plots of ground were considered gardens and how they were used. Do characteristics of past gardens appear in heaven's horticulture, and if so, can we speculate about which world is influencing which? Swedenborg reassures us that at some level the two worlds are indistinguishable, which would include their gardens. This observation, however, seems to apply to threshold experiences. As people take up life in the other world, initial familiarity makes way for spiritual reality, until eventually the memory of natural life recedes. Swedenborg says that in heaven externals 'are not wholly rejected and consigned to death, so as to become nothing', but rather are made subservient to interior things, and thus to the Lord Himself, and that these 'subserviences' are represented 'by colours [...] by odours, as of flowers'.[1] Paradoxically, the scents, sights, and textures of heavenly gardens—their sensual dimension—recall earthly gardens at the same time that they remind us of the proper subordination of externals to internals, of earth to heaven.

I would guess that heavenly gardens are grounded in peoples' memories and ideas of earthly gardens, but that heavenly gardens gradually exceed earthly concepts, becoming increasingly vibrant by way of contrast, first to what angels had experienced in a previous life, and later, to what they experienced in earlier states in heaven. The natural world, we are reminded throughout Swedenborg's works, flows from the spiritual world. But we are also told that the spiritual world—a vast realm of consciousnesses—is supplemented daily by new arrivals, thus new consciousnesses, from the natural world. It would seem then that the influence continues to flow both ways, though it is hard to fathom the intricacies of interaction. What does it mean to enter a 'familiar' world that is constantly in flux? How does the projection of each individual's internal state onto his or her surroundings fit with the human need for stable communities and environments? Swedenborg's descriptions of the afterlife create all sorts of practical and largely unanswered questions about geography, direction, time and space, but in one of his later works he suggests that although plants in heaven answer to the affections of the angels so that angels 'actually see and recognise the nature of affections by reference to the plants, as if they were symbols', the *alteration* of plants to reflect altered affections takes place 'outside communities'. [2] So too in our earthly gardens we recognize changes from day to day, or morning to evening, but the *process* itself seems undetectable, a mystery too finely wrought for our eyes to uncover. Thus we enjoy order and a sense of stability in spite of continual change.

Looking at the history of gardening and then speculating about uses and values gives at best a partial or distorted view, limited as we are to the records that survive of the gardens that left an impression significant enough to be recorded. We know little of the private, humble gardens of illiterate and impoverished people. We know even less of the inspiration people may have taken from these lost gardens. Perhaps some eighteenth-century slave in Virginia grew bluebells and daisies amongst the potatoes and onions in the patch of dry earth behind the slave quarters, simply to bring forth something unaccountable and beautiful beyond the master's control. From a spiritual view, such a patch of ground may have mirrored heaven more than all the avenues of topiary and reflecting pools in Versailles. Without traces or records we can only imagine that myriads of humble gardens have etched the earth, like fleeting expressions passing over a face now turned from us.

We do know something, however, about the grand gardens of powerful people and empires. From these we can speculate about trends in gardening, at least amongst the classes that could afford to devote land to purposes other than food production. The historical view that follows draws upon Penelope Hobhouse and other garden scholars. [3] For the most part, I look at only a few characteristics of a handful of major phases of gardening, drawing connections to Swedenborg as I see them, and offering here and there suggested resources for further study and reflection.

The ancient Middle East

The story of Western gardening goes back at least as far as the ancient worlds of Mesopotamia, the Middle East, Egypt and Persia.[4] People living in these regions became civilized, historians argue, through the process itself of becoming gardeners. In about 6000 BCE nomadic hunters began settling down to become farmers. 2,000 years later, the descendants of these first farmers, the Sumerians, came down from the uplands to the Tigris and Euphrates delta. Within another 1,000 years they had developed drainage and irrigation systems capable of turning swamps and desert into a 'fertile crescent'. A few hundred years later there were hunting parks with exotic plants and animals carried home from distant lands. This revolution of new techniques and new plants created a hierarchy of wealth and culture—a condition that Hobhouse sees as 'a key prerequisite of gardening'.[5] As non-utilitarian and aesthetic attitudes developed, horticulture became possible. This view of the development of horticulture as the movement *beyond* the merely utilitarian phase of food or medicine provides an interesting contrast to Swedenborg's view of heavenly horticulture, whose aesthetic quality always flows from useful function.

The claim that earthly horticulture was first made possible by the accumulation of wealth and culture perhaps suggests why gardens often register both the advancements and the declines of civilizations. Wealth and education foster the creation, display and appreciation of art and beauty. But the display of art can also parade as power and further inflate ego; concentrated wealth and refinement can lead to corruption and excess. In Christian imagery, the sensual snake easily dominates and destroys the spiritual garden. In Swedenborgian imagery, this snake, or sensual dimension of life, is not to be expelled but rather lifted up in service to higher values, as Moses takes hold of the serpent and, lifting it up, finds a staff in his hand. [6] The history of gardening provides a fascinating text for studying the changing uses of gardens, especially the ability or inability of various civilizations to stay focused on higher fruit.

If the historical development of horticulture on earth came about, in part, because of accumulations or even excesses of wealth, power and resources, the story of gardens in heaven is quite different, according to Swedenborg. Spiritual gardens spring spontaneously and directly from states of mind and heart. They manifest the perfect balance of love and wisdom, which is always a picture of usefulness. There are no excesses in heaven, no conspicuous consumption. Even the palaces, feasts and riches, described at times in almost childlike or fairy-tale imagery, are the outgrowth of actual uses being performed. No leisure classes. Days are structured around work and productivity, followed by relaxation. [7] Though we might not like the eighteenth-century, gem-encrusted finery that appears at times in Swedenborg's descriptions of heaven, we can be assured that our heavenly homes and surroundings will reflect our own tastes and be similarly off-putting to visitors from other eras. The fact that so much of the time Swedenborg is at a loss for words to convey what he sees in heaven suggests that the realities there exceed human language and conception. These scenes are not *excesses* of what we already have on earth; they are rather realities for which we have no mental or verbal containers. For example, Swedenborg describes the 'absolute and inexpressible joy' of heavenly paradise as arising from 'the most delicate, and humanly imperceptible, or sublime, mental imagery [. . .] in endless variation [. . .] so alive as to surpass, by leagues beyond number, any that a person on earth is able to picture to himself, or even think up'. Ultimately, 'the words are lacking, to be able to express these matters'. [8] Not only Swedenborg but the inhabitants of these gardens lack language and imagery to convey the experience of paradise: 'they who had been there were saying, as those who are there are saying now, that it is altogether so unutterable that they cannot present its ineffability even by the richest human mental image'. [9] Perhaps Swedenborg leaves many things undescribed, or minimally so, because he did not want to half-convey the external manifestation without the living experience of the use that called it forth, just as the angels themselves are unwilling to dwell on externals. Swedenborg claims that no wise person who enters heaven keeps his eyes fixed very long on the magnificent images there, 'but in his mind attends to the uses, since these delight in wisdom'. [10] Beauty certainly provides a use, especially on earth where we need to be inspired towards and reminded of higher things. In heaven, however, beauty flows from use, as an effect more than a cause.

Ancient Egypt

Moving from the Tigris and Euphrates delta to the Nile valley we see similar developments in horticulture, but generally on a more modest scale. In ancient Egypt, in contrast to the sprawling hunting parks of the Sumerians and Assyrians, planting was restricted for the most part to smaller areas, walled in and protected from the yearly flooding of the Nile. [11] Though less grand than some, these gardens had widespread influence on later horticulture. Various features of the garden designs of ancient Egypt surface all over the world, across time, in trellises, trained vines, terraces, tiled walls, sunken gardens, fish ponds, bird motifs, geometric lines and twinned features of all sorts. The architecture of the Greek peristyle and of monastic cloisters can be traced back to the Egyptian garden with its row of trees (columns) along an inner wall and overhanging branches (projecting rafters) to shade an enclosed courtyard. [12]

Ancient Egyptians planted gardens for all sorts of uses: pleasure, medicine, food, worship, shade and coolness. They had the first botanic gardens, and Pharaohs sometimes recorded amongst their great deeds the creation of gardens and the collection of exotic plants from far-off places. [13] We know something of the design and content of these various gardens from wall paintings, tomb reliefs, and documents, and from the analysis of pollen grains in mud bricks and plant remains in tombs. [14]

Symmetry was the most important feature of Egyptian gardens. With their straight lines, square corners, evenly spaced rows and twin trees at the centre, these gardens were the picture of formal, ordered and enclosed space. Even the ponds were rectangular. Softening this symmetry were all manner of fruits, vines, trees, and herbs, with the herbs geared to medicine, cooking, and cosmetics. In domestic gardens, flowers were carefully propagated—poppies, cornflowers, hollyhocks, lilies, mallows and mandrakes [15]—and used not only to decorate the home and adorn the body but to pay tribute to the gods. In New Kingdom times (1570-1070 BCE) these domestic gardens often included a bower where a woman in labour could find relief in the scented shade and cooler air. [16] It was thus not unusual for ancient Egyptians to be born in gardens and first open their eyes on an image of paradise.

With regard to Egypt's more public or grand gardens, some of the most beautiful were the painted ones on the walls of tombs and temples. Such artistic renderings leave a powerful record of the gardens which did not themselves survive. Temple gardens produced flowers and plants for embalming or for gifts to the gods, while royal gardens often consisted of extensive avenues of sacred trees. All trees in fact were sacred in Egypt, and with the expansion of botanical knowledge and the acquisition of specimens from around the world, 'the large variety of imported exotics made it possible for each temple to have its own sacred species'. [17] These collections of sacred trees, established to honour gods, gradually attested as well to the power of rulers who could collect, plant, and sustain ranks of trees in a desert climate.

The association of particular flowers, fruits, and trees with particular gods, and eventually with human rulers, reflects in interesting ways Swedenborg's view of the gradual distortion of the 'knowledge of correspondences' handed down from most ancient people. In their un-fallen state, these people knew that everything in the natural world reflected aspects of the *one* God, and they passed this knowledge, according to Swedenborg, to the ancient Egyptians:

among the Ancients there was the science of correspondences, which is also the science of representatives, *the* science of the wise. This was especially cultivated in Egypt, and is the source of the Egyptian hieroglyphics. From this science they knew the signification of animals of every kind, also the signification of trees of every kind, and of mountains, hills, rivers and fountains, and also of the sun, moon and stars; and as all their worship was representative, consisting wholly of correspondences, they celebrated it on mountains and hills, and also in groves and gardens. For the same reason they also regarded fountains as holy, and in their adoration of God they turned their faces to the rising sun. Moreover, they made graven images of horses, oxen, calves, lambs and also of birds, fishes and serpents, and set them up in their houses and other places in an order according to the spiritual things of the Church to which they corresponded or which they represented. They also placed similar objects in their temples that they might bring to remembrance the holy things which they signified. [18]

Gradually, however, the images began to be worshipped as multiple gods rather than multiple qualities of one God. Referring to Old Testament passages (Gen. 13.10; Ezek. 31.8) Swedenborg says that before Egypt fell into idolatry and perverted this knowledge of correspondence it was compared to the garden of Eden. [19] Perhaps one of the telling expressions of this fall was the enslavement of labour to build monuments. As the worship of one god turned into the worship of many gods, and eventually the deification of human rulers as gods, slave labour was needed to erect stone pyramids as symbols of power and divinity. The natural world ceased to be its own self-evident temple. In symbolic terms, and from an Old Testament perspective, the land of Goshen, a once garden-like and fertile land, became the land of grief and forced labour. Instead of a river of life to water the soil and bring forth paradisal fruit, looming monuments to death rose from the ground. In some ways the cultivation of flowers, fruits, and groves for worship of too many gods, and eventually for the deification of mere mortals, along with the erection of stone edifices and overreaching tombs built upon the backs of slaves, can be seen as the closing of a gate to heavenly paradise. Swedenborg makes the interesting claim, however, that with the coming of Christ 'the gate from the earthly paradise to the heavenly was opened', and that it would be opened again, 'at [God's] Advent into glory'. [20] He thus saw his own writing about the meaning of the Bible and the 'second coming' of Christ as a reopening of the connection between earthly and spiritual paradises.

Gardens have long been associated with heaven or an afterlife, even before the three monotheistic traditions of Judaism, Christianity, and Islam developed their ideas of a Garden of Eden. The earliest known writing (cuneiform tablets from 4000 BCE, discovered in Mesopotamia) refers to an irrigated paradise producing fruit trees and green meadows. [21] Babylonian tablets (2700 BCE) give fragments of the Sumerian *Epic of Gilgamesh*, which sounds something like a cross between the biblical Eden and Coleridge's 'Kubla Khan':

> And lo! the *gesdin* [Tree of life and immortality] shining stands,
> With crystal branches in the golden sands,
> In this immortal garden stands the tree,
> With trunk of gold, and beautiful to see.
> Beside a sacred fount the tree is placed,
> With emeralds and unknown gems is graced,
> Thus stands, the prince of emeralds, Elam's tree,
> As once it stood, gave Immortality
> To man, and bearing fruit, there sacred grew,
> Till Heaven claimed again Fair Eridu [Garden of Eden]. [22]

Most of these ancient traditions and texts that associate paradise with heaven also associate paradise with leisure. The idealization of doing nothing that characterizes many views of heaven suggests a distortion of the concept of 'effortless' labour, as Swedenborg describes the joyful activity of the earliest people who turned their lives towards God. Unlike escapist visions of heaven as a leisure garden, gardens on earth demand hard work. They always have. Dating back thousands of years BCE, a fragment of Egyptian verse describes the gardener's life as relentless toil:

> The gardener carries a yoke
> His shoulders are bent as with age:
> There's a swelling on his neck
> And it festers.
> In the morning he waters vegetables,
> The evening he spends with his herbs,
> While at noon he has toiled in the orchard.
> He works himself to death
> More than all the other professions. [23]

Ancient gardens as images of a work-free paradise were often built, ironically, through slave labour. At this level they paradoxically embody the loss of heaven on earth because enslaving others for one's own glory signals a fall, whereas serving others for God's sake brings freedom and rest.

Although the shape, scale, and produce of the gardens of ancient Egypt, Persia and Mesopotamia differ greatly from our modern Western gardens, especially in the ways that the flowers and trees often carried religious symbolism and were used in religious rituals, these ancient gardens prepared the way for future gardens. The gardeners of the ancient Middle East left two legacies. The first was water management—ancient gardens were built around a central source of moving water that often irrigated the rest of the garden. In Egypt especially the development of irrigation and canal systems, often of geometric shape, became a model for other desert civilizations. The second legacy was the huge parks, particularly hunting parks of the Assyrians, Babylonians, and Persians, which influenced medieval royal gardens, eighteenth-century landscape gardens, and, closer to home, modern urban parks. [24]

Beyond the obvious influences of water and scale that come to us from these ancient gardens, we can speculate about the motives behind their construction. When people plant gardens they manipulate the ground to speak certain shapes, colours, and textures, as well as certain values. Did ancient gardeners shape their gardens to mirror deeper or higher realities, such as water to figure God's truth or mercy, broad vistas to express freedom, and exotic plants and animals to represent the bounty of creation, or in Swedenborgian terms, the varieties of thought and love? Did the gardens perhaps merely reflect what these ancient desert civilizations lacked—water, shade, and colour? Did the lack of leisure in a daily struggle for subsistence make inactivity seem heavenly? More darkly, might the most grandiose of these gardens bear witness to the distorted values by which domination and pride of possession displace humility and human scale? Whatever these ancient gardens meant to their creators, or for whatever reasons they were constructed, we can learn about ourselves by trying to read them, and especially by trying to understand what seems lasting and beautiful in the ways humans establish and interact with gardens. Learning about the gardens of other people and other civilizations can inform our own efforts to create both physical and symbolic beauty and order. The gardens we envision and build embody and promote the values we cherish, whether it be beauty, ingenuity, community, reflection, worship, wonder, humility, meditation or simple appreciation for the cycles of life and our own place in them.

Ancient Greek and Roman gardens

The Greeks and Romans shaped the development of horticulture as both an art and a science, allowing us to draw inspiration from their knowledge and practices, and lessons from their excesses.

Although Greece is too arid for lavish garden displays, it was the birthplace of botany. Greece has more flowering plants and ferns than any other European country—more than 6,000 species, according to Hobhouse.[25] The Greeks emphasized primarily the medicinal and other practical uses of plants. As early as the 8th century BCE Homer was describing plants, but predominantly the useful ones. By the 5th century BCE Hippocrates had developed practical medicine. Aristotle continued the study of plants in the next century, followed by his student Theophrastus, whose classification of over 450 plants provided the basis of modern botany. When Theophrastus died he freed his slaves, with the coda that they continue to maintain the garden.[26] This mandate to work the garden presents, ironically, the idea of a certain kind of labour as itself the sustaining condition of freedom—an interesting turn to the idea of sweating in the fields as a sign of the Fall.

One of the most interesting uses of gardens in ancient Greece was as settings for education and philosophical debate. Robert Pogue Harrison, in his *Gardens: An Essay on the Human Condition* (2008), explores the appropriateness of garden settings as teaching sites for Socrates and Plato, especially for the fruitful dialogue and dialectic that shaped their exchanges with students and disciples. [27] The art of conversation, Harrison claims, was fostered in the garden spaces that were the ancient academies. This conversation in gardens, generally outside the city walls, lies at the heart of intellectual freedom, humanism and a healthy republic, as Harrison describes it:

> Conversation is as essential to learning as it is to the life of the republic, for republicanism, as the civic humanists understood it, is all about a plurality of voices making themselves heard in an open forum. The exchange of opinion—even where the matter is not political in content, and even when it takes place in a private garden—is the best defense against unreasoned prejudice and blind ignorance, for it refers opinions to the claims of reason, which is the natural enemy of arbitrary tyranny. Discussion, debate, and deliberation are the means by which the citizens exercise their judicious wisdom in a republic. [28]

The civic humanism that would be born later in Renaissance Italy through revived study of Roman and Greek writers had its roots in just such garden dialogue and philosophy. It is perhaps not surprising that

Swedenborg, an eighteenth-century scholar thoroughly schooled in the classics and in humanist values, would envision, in his work, the primary setting and mode of education in the spiritual world as comprising debates and dialogues in outdoor forums and garden settings.

Much as the Romans built upon Greek philosophy and civilization, so they would build on Greek knowledge of plants and gardens. Pliny the Elder's *Naturalis Historia*, which used Greek sources to compile all known knowledge of the natural world, remained the great dictionary of botanical knowledge throughout the Middle Ages. Although the Romans drew heavily from the Greeks, including the design of their small domestic gardens,[29] they developed large-scale gardening far more rapidly and lavishly than the Greeks, in large part because of improved technology. The Greeks had depended on natural springs; the Romans built aqueducts and plumbing. Pools and fountains appeared everywhere. Irrigation systems supported a wide range of plants culled from far-reaching territories. As the Roman empire grew, the gardens became grander, until the 'vast pleasure gardens', and a related neglect of agriculture and over-dependence on imported products, came to epitomize, ironically, the empire's failing infrastructure.[30]

By the first century BCE so much attention was being directed to Roman pleasure gardens and so little to agriculture that critics began to praise 'the good old days when farming used to be held in high esteem'.[31] Not only were pleasure gardens filling up the countryside where open space provided an empty palette but urban gardens began to expand vertically. Roofs were 'laid out with pergolas, ornamental plants, and fountains', and larger gardens were 'supported on masonry in mid-air', leading Seneca to lament the unnaturalness of such gardeners: 'Live not they against nature that plant orchards on their highest towers, that have whole forests shaking upon the tops and turrets of their houses, spreading their roots in such places where it would suffice them that the tops of their branches should touch?' [32] It was the very overblown and artificial nature of these Roman gardens in the third century (much like the English gardens in the eighteenth century) that led to parodies of such garden excess. Horace and Martial satirized the excesses of the classical world, while Alexander Pope (1688-1744) was the most outspoken critic of the vulgarity of eighteenth-century garden design. [33]

As excess and ornamentation replaced restraint and utility, Rome began to decay. Ironically, these very ruins would seduce later centuries to replicate Roman grandeur and to romanticize decay. During the Renaissance, Europe studied the ruins of Roman villas and gardens, copied layouts, and relocated statues to ornament its own gardens, all in hopes of emulating the aura of magnificence and power. But before the Renaissance (beginning in Italy) resuscitated the classical world, Europe experienced an age of disinterest in or distrust of the natural world. During these centuries much of the knowledge of botany and gardening *seemed* to disappear, although it was actually safe and even thriving elsewhere. As gardeners know, soil can exhaust itself, and when it does, it is good for certain seasons to allow the ground to lie fallow. In terms of gardening, Europe lay mostly fallow during this time between the fall of the Roman empire and the rise of the Renaissance. While Europe slept in the west, the gardens of Islam bloomed in the east.

Islamic gardens

Eastern gardens focused on both earthly delight and heavenly beauty. Interwoven elements of protective walls, running water, symmetry, shade, trees and spaces for peaceful reflection characterize Muslim gardens of all sorts. Although Islamic teachings restricted image-making, ornamentation was permitted, especially floral and vegetable motifs. Writing too was used to decorate surfaces, especially calligraphy quoting the Koran. 'This ornamentation was applied to all surfaces', Hobhouse says, 'as a reminder of heaven in all aspects of life'. [34] The reliance on quotations from the Koran as an integral part of garden design makes a powerful backdrop to Swedenborg's spiritual descriptions of gardens *as* the Word, and of the Word appearing *in* gardens in heaven. Most characteristically, Muslim gardens were based on water and symmetry, the gardens being generally rectangular, enclosed within walls, and divided into four sections by four waterways representing the four rivers of life: water, milk, wine and honey. [35] Because of the division into four sections these gardens are called *chahar bagh* (Farsi for 'four gardens'). One of the greatest appeals of the Islamic garden was its walled-in privacy and peaceful seclusion, a spiritual oasis from the press of everyday life.

In many ways the quietness and privacy of Islamic gardens stands in startling contrast to the development of showy, public gardens in the West, where the opportunity to parade and be seen in one's finery was not the least of the garden's appeal. Though Genghis Khan (in the thirteenth century) and his descendants destroyed much that was sacred and beautiful in the Eastern world, much survived, especially through Muslim control and influence over southern Spain from the eighth century. The Moors, as the Muslim peoples who conquered and occupied parts of Spain were often called, brought exquisite gardens, mosaics and architecture, as well as many new species of plants to Europe. They also reintroduced the lost botanical knowledge of the Greeks and the gardening technology of the Romans. The Alhambra palace, built in the mid-fourteenth century in the city of Granada, beautifully articulates in plants, water, arch and mosaic this Muslim aesthetic. Other examples abound, many from sixteenth- and seventeenth-century gardens that have been partially or wholly restored, each reflecting the divine in some combination of features. A description of several of these gardens follows.

Bagh-e Fin in Esfahan, Iran is a sixteenth-century Persian *chahar bagh* whose water enters the garden from the north and flows into turquoise-tiled channels to a shaded central pavilion where the water comes to rest, 'silent [. . .] in square basins like mirrors open to the sky, as though to receive the heavens into a place that excites the imagination as a union of the earthly and the divine'.[36] In another garden, underground aqueducts carry precious water—'the symbol of God's mercy'—22 miles from the Shirkuh mountains to cool the ground of Bagh-e Doulatabad in Yazd, Iran.[37] Jahangir's Tomb Garden in Punjab,

Pakistan is a seventeenth-century Islamic-Mughal design with marble and semi-precious stone inlay of floral motifs and canals and trees radiating out to four gatehouses. [38] Other gardens served as schools of astrology, such as Pari Mahal (Kashmir, India) whose seven terraces represented the seven known planets. [39] And one final example, Bagh-i Hayat Bakhsh (Delhi, India), a Mughal *chahar bagh* conceived as 'a symbol of good government, a terrestrial image of paradise, described in the Koran as ''gardens underneath which rivers flow'' '. [40] These beautiful remnants, along with descriptions of exquisite gardens that have not survived, give some inkling of the peaceful beauty of Islamic gardens with their carefully constructed waterways, geometric lines, shade, stone inlay, fretwork, filigree screens and carefully placed carpets for rest and reflection. Not only were there carpets laid in the gardens, but garden designs were woven into the carpets. Beyond physical gardens, Islamic influence comes through garden *motifs* sewn into tapestries, painted on silk and paper, woven into clothing and rugs, fired into tiles and patterned in mosaic walls, floors and ceilings.

It is certainly strange that as entire civilizations are rising and disappearing, aspects of their influence extend subtly but inexorably through gardens and plants. Rome thought to conquer Greece but was shaped in turn by Greek philosophy, horticulture and art. The Islamic and Christian faiths battled one another at every turn, perhaps most blatantly in the Crusades to 'liberate' the Holy Land from the clutch of infidels, but it was the Europeans who were captivated by exotic flowers, trees and gardens. As a result of the Crusades, 'the damask rose and carnation entered the gardens and tapestries of the Western world and the pomegranate, lemon and orange trees were planted on the northern shore of the Mediterranean'.[41] The design of Islamic gardens remains embedded to this day in Western gardens.[42] Similarly, the horticulture of the Americas would reshape conquering Europe. Europe assumed it mastered the new world by planting flags and redrawing maps, but the potato, tomato and corn planted their own lasting claim on the old world. No less at the level of the personal and the individual than at the level of rising and waning civilizations, plants and gardens cultivate the people who think to cultivate them.

Medieval gardens

For the millennium between the decline of Rome to the rise of the Renaissance (400-1400), we know little about gardening in Europe, except that it centred on monastery and castle gardens. There are idealized views of paradise and gardens in religious art, particularly paintings and tapestries, but little is known about gardens in the ground. Northern Europe with its cold, dark climate was not fertile ground for lush gardens. Only a few descriptions of gardens remain. One of these is a drawing of a layout for a monastery garden from 820 CE, depicting a cemetery, herbs, medicinal plants, vegetables in rectangular plots, and a flower bed in an area labelled 'paradise'.[43] Rather modest and unassuming, monastic gardens were designed to meet the needs of monks and travellers. At first these gardens did not have a specific healing focus. By the sixth century, however, monks were not only permitted but even encouraged by the church to specialize in healing. And by the late Middle Ages the herb gardens emphasized curative plants. These curative and subsistence gardens gradually created allowances for aesthetic components as well, thus driving a wedge into the ascetic mindset of the Middle Ages.

In Britain, the coming of the Benedictine monk Augustine to Canterbury (597 CE) revived attention to the civilization, art and letters that had fallen by the way during the centuries of tribal conflict that ensued when Rome withdrew from Britain. Although they began as humble places of retreat and self-sufficiency, cultivated communally by the monks, monastery gardens in Britain gradually expanded into larger gardens with more varied produce, in part because the Benedictine emphasis on 'work sanctified by prayer [as] the best thing a man can do' [44] dignified and validated toil in gardens. The gardens got bigger and began to produce not just vegetables for food and herbs for healing but even flowers for worship and beauty. The flowers that were once despised by the early Christians because of their association with paganism and idolatry were now grown 'to decorate the church'. [45] Although medieval gardens were never cultivated *primarily* for aesthetic purposes, there was at least some movement away from the ascetic drive to manifest faith by self-denial and barren surroundings. In 1530, for instance, the Abbot of Liessies encouraged his monks to 'enjoy the pleasure of gardening but without ownership', and to allow the beauties of nature to draw the soul to God:

May the beauty of flowers and other creatures draw the heart
To love and admire God, their creator,
May the garden's beauty bring to mind the splendour of paradise. [46]

In addition to the beauty of flowers focusing attention on paradise and God, the seclusion of gardens and cloistered spaces represented 'the contemplation into which the soul withdraws itself and hides, after being separated from the crowd of carnal thoughts'. The middle of the cloister with its grass plot known as 'paradise' signified the 'greenness' of the monks' virtues. [47] The medieval garden thus was a sermon of sorts, drawing attention to God's bounty and discouraging self-aggrandizement.

The medieval garden gradually developed from a kitchen plot to a healing bed, and cautiously, to a space for instruction and inspiration. Certainly the short growing season of western and northern Europe affected the output of the gardens, but more than climate, religion seems to have circumscribed the horticultural vision. Above all, a mistrust of the senses and the natural world kept gardens understated in the Middle Ages, not just monastery gardens but others as well. Edith Wharton (1862-1937) describes the garden of the Middle Ages, by way of contrast to the grand Italian Renaissance gardens, as a 'mere patch of ground within the castle precincts, where "simples" [herbs] were grown around a central well-head and fruit was espaliered against the walls'. [48] Though simple and understated, these gardens were not unimportant. Wharton identifies them as precursors to the Renaissance gardens, especially in the way that they mediated between the interior space of the dwelling and the countryside beyond. As castle walls were thrown down and gardens expanded, 'taking in the fish-pond, the bowling green, the rose arbour and the clipped walk', [49] then the medieval garden was well on its way to becoming the Renaissance garden. [50] The most important feature in this outward expansion from the castle garden to the estate garden was the view of the landscape, a perspective that drew attention outward, not inward. Such a shift in perspective is a good metaphor as well for the increased secularization of gardens as they expanded beyond the introspective focus of the church-dominated Middle Ages.

The most important and most extravagant gardens of the medieval period were not gardens in the ground but gardens in the imagination and in art. Perhaps art, especially in service of the church, was seen as a safe remove from the physical world. In paintings, gardens appeared as backgrounds to New Testament events, 'with lilies, roses, potted plants or topiary identifying events or individuals and triple-tiered estrades symbolizing the Trinity'. [51] In architecture and textiles, complex foliage symbolism was carved into stone and woven into tapestries. In literature, there were allegorical gardens and *horti deliciarum*, or Gardens of Eden, at every turn. In poems such as *Pearl* (late fourteenth century) the action takes place in a garden, and in Malory's *Le Morte d'Arthur* (1485) a flowery woodland space sets the stage. *Le Roman de la rose*, written in the first half of the thirteenth century, vividly depicts English and French gardens in the Middle Ages, including flowery mead, fruit trees, stone-coped beds, clipped shrubs, plants in beds and containers, central fountains, surrounding walls and moats. [52] These allegorical gardens are similar in many ways to their monastic counterparts in being walled in and protected from a corrupting world, but unlike the monastery gardens with their emphasis on food production, healing and human activity, these imagined paradises are curiously static and unattainably perfect, much like the Christian visions of heaven during this age.

Gardens in medieval art represent idealized views, perhaps nowhere realized in soil and sun. They tell us much, however, about the *desire* for retreat, safety and beauty, for a paradisal respite from a world that was frequently overwhelmed by illness, poverty, natural disasters and political strife. One never knew when fire or earthquake would demolish a town, or plague or war would devastate a countryside. Idealized and highly artificial views of paradise as enclosed gardens with tamed animals and trained plants, all arranged in predictable and pleasing patterns, brought geometric stability and other-worldly comfort. The allegorical garden, however, was not entirely enclosed and self-sufficient. Hobhouse speaks of the 'magical enclosed space' of the garden proper in the allegories of *Le Roman de la rose*, Boccaccio, and Chaucer but argues that there are always references to an outer garden, 'that *locus amoenus* of woodland glades or flower-filled fields where the garden was unstructured and free'. [53] The idea of an outer garden that is less defined or contained anticipates landscape gardens of the eighteenth century. Landscape gardens would emphasize nature and the horizon instead of a life sequestered from the physical world. It is almost as if the pressing of boundaries had to be rehearsed in artistic and literary

imaginations before being put into practice. Swedenborg's descriptions
of gardens in heaven (see Part II) resemble these allegorical gardens
in the way they balance tightly controlled horticulture and enclosures
against curving avenues and ambiguous boundaries, as if modelling
a play between control and order on the one hand, and innovation
and self-expression on the other.

Renaissance gardens

The enclosed garden of the Middle Ages becomes more expansive,
open and ornate in the Renaissance as new (or classically old) ideas of
proportion and perspective and the interaction between form and landscape begin to shape new gardens. There is a sense in the Renaissance
of renewed delight in the natural world, quite different from the
guarded attitudes towards pleasure and nature that characterized the
Christian temper of the Middle Ages. The garden in the Renaissance
becomes a place for outdoor socializing and, as in the ancient gardens,
for intellectual debate. Hobhouse informs us that early Renaissance
gardens were 'subdivided into separate but regular parts by pergolas
and hedges'. They were based on a 'grid system defined by perspective',
where everything was carefully aligned and clipped, and where the
'garden "outside" was an architectural extension of the "inside"'.[54]
There was an apparent manipulation of nature. The repetition of
design and order aimed to create a balance between human control
imposed from the outside and divine order emanating from the inside.
'Art imitates nature', Hobhouse goes on to say, 'by repeating artificially

what nature put there naturally'. [55] This imitation was addressed not just to the external appearance but also to 'underlying if elusive pre-ordained order'. And beyond imitation of external and internal order, there was the Renaissance belief that 'nature could be improved by the gardener's art'. [56] In the best sense, the garden would highlight divine order through the beauty of classical perspective and the harmony of line in house, garden and surrounding landscape. [57] This attention to line and perspective in Renaissance gardens eventually became overdone, even slavish, as the Renaissance progressed and as gardens became places to display and impose authority as much as to uncover inherent harmony. The landscape architect Ian McHarg (1921-2001) describes such gardens as spaces where 'the authority of man was made visible by the imposition of a simple Euclidean geometry upon the landscape [...]. Man imposes his simple, entertaining illusion of order, accomplished with great art, upon an unknowing and uncaring nature'. [58] Nowhere was this obsessive control of nature more obvious and overblown than in seventeenth-century French royal gardens.

The French formal gardens of Louis XIV with their clipped hedges, arbour alleys, waterworks and geometric designs, grandly illustrate human control over nature, and a monarch's control over his empire. The gardens at Versailles, Marly, and St Cloud were created to impress and intimidate the viewer. In the century that followed Louis XIV, as gardening became more attuned to nature, critics like the nobleman and garden designer René-Louis de Girardin (1735-1808) looked back on such seventeenth-century displays of wealth and power as grotesquely *inartistic*. Girardin castigates André Le Nôtre, master garden designer for Louis XIV, for his many offences against nature:

> The famous Le Nôtre, who lived in the last age, contributed to the destruction of nature by subjecting everything to the compass; the only ingenuity required, was measuring with a ruler, and drawing lines like the cross-bars of a window; then followed the planta- tion according to the rules of symmetry; the ground was laid smooth at great expense, the trees were mutilated and tortured in all ways, water shut up within four walls, the view confined by massy hedges, and the prospect from the house limited to a flat parterre, cut out into squares like a chess board, where the glittering sand and gravel of all colors, only dazzled and fatigued the eyes; so that the nearest way to get out of this dull scene, soon became the most frequented path. [59]

In this same century, Abbé Jacques de Lille's poem *The Garden* (1782) suggests a deepening respect for *natural* gardens, and by extension, for natural or common humanity:

> Would you adorn the simply-charming plain,
> Insult not Nature, with a gaudy train.
> The talk requires a deep prophetic mind,
> A genius, not a fortune unconfin'd;

Less proud, than elegant; for pomp and show,
Let simple beauties 'mid thy gardens grow.
[. . .] But ere you plant, ere yet your impious spade
The sacred bosom of the earth invade,
To make your garden wear a juster face,
Know Nature, watch and imitate her grace.
[. . .] Let not dull symmetry your lawn confine;
'Tis liberty gives life to each design. [60]

Composed just seven years before the fall of the Bastille, and sixteen years before the publication of Coleridge and Wordsworth's *Lyrical Ballads*, this unassuming garden poem with its affirmation of liberty and nature subtly anticipates the political revolution near at hand in France, and the poetic revolution in England that would internalize that energy to create a new order of the imagination.

The Renaissance fascination with manipulating the natural world for display can be seen, perhaps, as an expression of overconfidence in human knowledge and power to produce whatever effects are desired. Swedenborg parodies spirits in the other world who proudly display their ability to use reason to manipulate truth, using teachings from the Word to prove whatever they desire. These spirits appear to themselves in grand surroundings, which disintegrate when the vapid nature of their arguments is revealed. Given Swedenborg's willingness to critique prideful or self-serving displays of intellect, it seems odd that Louis XIV, the regal power behind the grand and ornate Renaissance gardens at

Versailles, comes across quite favourably to Swedenborg in the spiritual world. [61] Although it is tempting to read a garden as pompous as Versailles as the manifestation of an inflated ego, Swedenborg gives little support for such a reading, both from what he says about Louis XIV, and from his teaching that in earthly life internals cannot be judged by externals, not even in ourselves. The meanings we find in other people's gardens are best limited, perhaps, to whatever applications make our own ground more fruitful.

Looking across the Channel from France to Tudor, Elizabethan and Jacobean England (sixteenth and seventeenth centuries) we find the manipulation of gardens and landscapes far less pronounced than in Renaissance Europe, especially France. But there were exceptions, of course, and some of the best illustrations of the excesses of garden design, along the Renaissance model, can be seen in the *parodies* of the great English pleasure gardens with their pretentious designs and slavish imitation of classical features. No poet was a more merciless critic than Alexander Pope, though even the scathing critic could not resist building a grotto in his own garden. In general, English gardens were more attuned and adapted to the surrounding landscape than were the French gardens, probably taking some of their influence from across the Atlantic where vast natural landscapes and the sublime power of wilderness were shaping a new consciousness.

The great English landscape gardens of the eighteenth century drew nature in rather than walled it out. Lakes, meadows, rolling hills and artfully grouped trees were incorporated into the painterly purview of the landscape garden. Instead of walls and hedges to distinguish the garden from the world outside, the landscape garden erased boundaries, emphasizing 'the natural' as an underlying aesthetic principle. Of course nature was not untouched in the landscape garden, only made to appear so. The depiction of nature was an idealized, almost pastoral or bucolic view, reaching back in some ways to the classical gardens of Greece and Rome, which were themselves nostalgic for some lost idealized state. The concept of Eden, which has been around as long as humans have kept records, has generally been an idealized, often highly artificial, view of lost innocence. One sign of being fallen people, ironically, is that we are conscious of loss and thus look backwards. The un-fallen most ancient people, who according to Swedenborg lived in garden surroundings in close communication with heaven, did not need a concept of Eden to sustain them. It is only we nostalgic latecomers who need to think our way back to an unselfconscious experience of the natural world.

The English landscape garden of the eighteenth century would seem to move towards egalitarian views of gardening, switching emphasis from the highly wrought centre to the seemingly untouched and natural periphery. But like the slave labour hidden behind the serene surface of the ancient gardens, or the drive to manifest power behind the clipped acres of Renaissance gardens, the eighteenth-century landscape gardens embody their own subtle form of decadence. Landscape gardens require enormous tracts of land, many of which were taken through the land enclosure acts that privatized common land. Wealthy aristocrats now had more canvas on which to paint their landscape designs, but commoners lost their fields and livelihoods. The British poet Oliver Goldsmith describes this betrayal of one class by another in *The Deserted Village* (1770):

> While scourged by famine from the smiling land,
> The mournful peasant leads his humble band;
> And while he sinks, without one arm to save,
> The country blooms—a garden, and a grave.
>
> Where then, ah, where shall poverty reside,
> To 'scape the pressure of contiguous pride?
> If to some common's fenceless limits stray'd,
> He drives his flock to pick the scanty blade,
> Those fenceless fields the sons of wealth divide,
> And even the bare-worn common is deny'd. [62]

Goldsmith's view of rural life is itself idealized and nostalgic, but clearly enclosure laws, along with the lure of urban centres, helped bring a new generation into the cities, where a combination of industrial growth, population explosion, and a lack of city planning would create a new face to poverty and suffering. And in the next century (nineteenth), urban poverty, overcrowding and squalor would remove people even further from the semblance of garden life, though the Romantic poets in England and the Transcendentalists in America would do their part to recover Eden through acts of poetic imagination. [63]

It is to eighteenth-century England that Swedenborg travelled to publish his theology. With its free and bustling press, [64] its coffee houses and conversations, its evolving view of landscape gardens as an interweaving of natural wildness and imposed order, and its devotion to reason and intellect, England was a fertile spot for new ideas. Swedenborg writes favourably of the English freedom to think, write and publish, claiming that such people occupy the centre of heaven. [65] He was in the right place at the right time to disseminate his work, which was itself largely concerned with spiritual freedom. But he was publishing in Neo-Latin, the learned but waning language of the Renaissance. Swedenborg got his works to England, but for the most part, not into English. [66] 250 years after Swedenborg left this world, uttering his final words in heavily accented English, [67] translators are still working to bring his ideas and fading Latin metaphors into modern English usage.

Swedenborg's era

During the century before Swedenborg's birth in 1688, 20 times as many plants entered Europe than in the previous 2,000 years. This era leading into the eighteenth century brought what Hobhouse calls a 'major shift' in the relationship between people and plants as the latter began to change people's lives and professions. [68] Botanists, writers, printers, artists, collectors, nurserymen and gardeners all dealt in the business of studying, depicting, growing and sharing plants. Swedenborg was born into an era ignited with interest in the physical world, eager to use science to probe the seemingly infinite specimens of life, and confident, even overconfident, in the power of reason to impose order and make sense of it all. The best example of the eighteenth-century drive to categorize the natural world into an orderly system was the Swedish botanist Linnaeus (Carl von Linné, 1707-78). Linnaeus wanted to classify and name every animal, plant and mineral. He developed a Latin-based binomial nomenclature to identify everything by genus and species. Not only did his system present an orderly way to identify and group plants and animals, it gave the world common terms for discussion. As plants crossed borders they retained universally recognized names, which greatly enhanced people's ability to study them and accumulate information.

Linnaeus provides an interesting foil for Swedenborg in several ways. The two men were related by marriage (Linnaeus married Swedenborg's cousin); they lived at about the same time (Swedenborg was 19 years older) and in the same city for many years; both were scientists publishing in Latin; and both were lovers of plants and kept gardens. But whereas Linnaeus gave us a binomial system to describe natural life, a system so useful it is still relied upon today, Swedenborg offered a trinomial system to explore spiritual reality. In Swedenborg's economy, all things could be divided into components of love and wisdom, or good and truth, but a crucial third term injects value and meaning—a thing's use or purpose. Swedenborg was an avid student of the physical world, but finding the natural plane incomplete, even insubstantial, he kept looking for a spiritual realm, for the spiritual reality behind physical reality. He argued that use or service calls all things into being, that everyone and everything exists to serve a purpose in an intricate divine plan that is fully realized in a spiritual realm. Unlike Linnaeus' famous forays into nature to collect specimens, Swedenborg could not bring back specimens of spiritual life to his laboratory, though he brought the language and methods of science to his theological writing. [69] He was a scientist grappling with spirit. Paradoxically, he claimed the evidence of his senses—'I have seen, I have heard' [70]—for phenomena that often could not be reduced to earthly expression, especially since spiritual phenomena were even less likely than natural phenomena to hold still. Linnaeus is a household name; Swedenborg is nearly unknown. We may find, however, that when we reach the spiritual realm Swedenborg's trinomial terms, with their emphasis on interaction, constant growth and change, might provide a helpful system for tracking spiritual life.

Swedenborg did not of course abandon this world for the next. Even while travelling in spirit he continued his work and interactions in this world. As far as can be determined from written accounts and stories, he was a good, wise and faithful man in his personal and professional life. In addition to several thorough studies of Swedenborg's life and work, [71] there are specific explorations of his garden. [72] I want to speculate briefly about what the garden says about the gardener Swedenborg, as well as the gardener in each of us.

Swedenborg's garden

When he was 55 years old (in 1743), having worked successfully in several disciplines, travelled widely and published broadly, Swedenborg bought a home and laid out a garden. Though he would not fully take up residence until two years later when he returned from one of his many trips abroad (1745), Swedenborg was ready to put down roots. During the two-year hiatus between buying ground and moving in, he received his spiritual call and devoted his life to writing down and publishing the truth revealed to him. It seems timely that at the moment he chose to settle most firmly on earth, buying property and planting seeds, he was himself being transplanted to another world.

One of the few records we have of the plants in Swedenborg's own garden comes from a 1752 almanac in which Swedenborg wrote notes in the margins indicating which pages of the *Arcana Caelestia* had been sent to the printer and, on the reverse side, a record of plants in his greenhouse: from artichokes and lemons to alliums and roses. [73] The squeezing of notation and lists into margins and blank spaces hints at thrift, while the interspersing of texts—practical almanac information, progress in publishing a work of spiritual exegesis, and the contents of garden beds—suggests a multilayered interest in life. Even far-off America shoulders its way into the picture. Elsewhere Swedenborg mentions the American colonies only in passing or in reference to their inaccessibility, yet the final garden notation in his 1752 almanac lists 'American seeds' growing in his garden: mulberry, melons, buttonwood, beech, dogwood and an unidentified 'pod-bearing tree'. [74]

Swedenborg's garden is both a powerful metaphor and solid ground. Most eighteenth-century gardens kept by scientists were used for study and experimentation. Swedenborg certainly studied and admired the plants in his garden, but his garden also blossomed with many other uses. He walked in it for the sheer pleasure of communion with nature, taking visitors along with him. He wrote theology in the garden, in a summer house situated at the west end of his property facing the garden, and he also worked the garden itself. One might expect an eighteenth-century aristocrat to delegate gardening to servants, but Swedenborg seems to have relished the physical labour and contact with the plants and earth, and he was happy to share the harvest. He was a generous landlord, allowing his gardener's family to profit from the fruits of the garden. Census records for the city of Stockholm indicate that when Swedenborg's servants retired they were remarkably well off.[75] Swedenborg's garden seems to have been one whose beauty did not come at some hidden expense or distortion. He shared the garden with visitors and children, building fanciful structures, such as mazes and mirrored gardens, to appeal to the imagination of the young, or the young at heart. He meditated in and on his garden, visiting it at various times of day. He went to the garden when distressed and needing to seek guidance. A friend of Swedenborg's in the Swedish diet once described Swedenborg's response to bad news as a retreat to his garden: 'Swedenborg was then very grieved but soon he went out into his garden, there he kneeled down praying to the Lord in tears, asking what he should do now? And he then got the consoling conviction that nothing evil would happen to him'.[76] Swedenborg's modest garden plot of just over an acre held plants from all over the world, and a variety of structures, pathways and beds (Fig. 3 overleaf). In

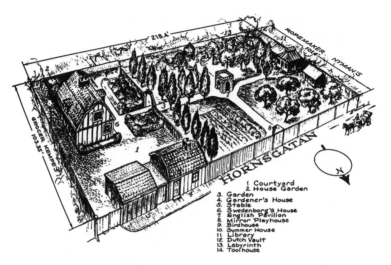

Fig. 3. Drawing of Swedenborg's garden by Donald Moorhead.

addition to vegetables, fruit trees, poplar and cypress, there were arrays of flowers: tulips, hyacinths, carnations, sweet peas, larkspur, violets, scabiosa, sweet william, Canterbury bells, catmint, chalcedonica, spurrey, lilies, sunflowers and roses of many varieties: African, Adonis, white, blue and velvet. There were stone paths and a tall enclosing fence, an ornate gate and an orchard, a kitchen garden, bird house, summer house, garden house, library, maze and a mirror creating the illusion of a doubled garden. [77] The garden was laid out along formal lines, but with eccentricities and flourishes, all nicely reflecting Swedenborg's own mind—open but protected, useful and abundant with life. [78]

Reproducing a drawing and a list of plants does little to recreate the experience of a garden, just as reading about correspondences is nothing like the actual experience of them. To know Swedenborg's garden we would have to stand under the arch and smell the lilies, roses, catmint and chamomile; watch the heavy sunflowers sway in the Swedish breeze, or the heads of tulips turn gently into the frail warmth of the northern sun; hear the soft thud of apples dropping on the ground; glimpse birds darting from beech to buttonwood to cypress; or trace the stumble of bees through pear pollen and mulberry stain. What is most spectacular, finally, about this nearly forgotten plot of sown ground that was Swedenborg's garden is its sheer commonness (see Appendix). The same plants grow in thousands of gardens across Europe and the United States, probably in our own garden, or the one next door. This is how close heaven lies. As far as we know, Swedenborg did not edit his garden to mirror the things he saw in heaven. He did not need to. All Swedenborg had to do was engage with the physical world from spiritual intent, and the locks sprung open on the treasure chests of meaning.

Afterword

S wedenborg planted a garden at about the time he turned all his talents and efforts to theology and spiritual experience. The garden manifested his commitment to homemaking; it provided a backdrop to meditation; and it served as a laboratory for inspiration. He wrote tirelessly of the correspondence of gardens in revelation, reiterating that the first garden represented a pure state of heart and mind, and all subsequent gardens represented the rational and intellectual capacity for recovery of that original state. He lived in an era when Europe was flooded with the plants of the rest of the world, and botany had become a scientific passion. He used these advances in knowledge about the physical world to corroborate divine nature. During the 27 years of his dual life in two worlds he visited hundreds of gardens in heaven and brought back tantalizing yet anaemic descriptions. If we fail to call upon our imagination when reading these descriptions we might not sense the presence of gardens at all, even though gardens are such a frequently recurring setting in heaven. On the other hand, the millions of gardens of the past are not particularly tangible either; even the best descriptions mean almost nothing if we have not some first-hand experience of gardens on which to draw.

Gardens are ephemeral, fragile things. They do not last, even from year to year. Each spring a new garden replaces the old one. By midsummer loved plants die or fail to thrive. Hardy survivors crowd out tentative growth. The sundials so common in gardens of all eras serve as constant reminders of time passing and nature cycling through life and death. Our own mortality surrounds us in a garden. But gardens are shining, joyful things as well. Our interaction with them connects us to healing rhythms across time and space. The very uncertainty of them is part of their joy; this uncertainty makes the planting of any garden an act of faith. Vita Sackville-West (1892-1962), gardener and writer, describes planting a white garden of pansies, peonies, and irises, in a context of green and grey leaves. But then she admits that since the garden may be 'a terrible failure' what she really wants is 'only to suggest that such experiments are worth trying'. She ends with the beautiful statement 'I cannot help hoping that the great ghostly barn owl will sweep silently across a pale garden, next summer, in the twilight—the pale garden that I am now planting, under the first flakes of snow'.[1] She never says 'my' garden. The hoped for owl will sweep across 'a' garden, 'the garden that [she] is now planting'. We own nothing but the effort to cooperate with the life that streams through nature. And in truth, even the effort is not our own.

Gardens are acts of faith and love and imagination, much like our own lives. To sink seeds and bulbs into dark earth at the edge of winter for the sake of beauty in a spring we may not witness is an extension of imagination and sympathy that leaves our own minds and hearts well sown. Like the poet Robert Frost positioned halfway up a ladder that is planted on the ground but with its top sticking through an apple tree 'toward heaven', we are positioned between worlds, where we take hold of ladders, or birch trees, or poetry, or music, or gardens, or any vehicle to carry us to the edge of things where we can become conscious of both our natural and spiritual natures.

To commune with nature, which is gardening at its best, is to identify with nature but also to transcend it. What truly blossoms in gardens, or in any humble rapport with nature, is human consciousness. In the final lines of *The Prelude*, a manifesto of Romantic poetry, Wordsworth addresses Coleridge as a fellow 'prophet of nature' and affirms the calling to inspire a love of nature for the sake of the healing power such love brings to elevate and strengthen consciousness:

[. . .] what we have loved,
Others will love, and we will teach them how;
Instruct them how the mind of man becomes
A thousand times more beautiful than the earth
On which he dwells [. . .] [2]

No one found the earth more beautiful than Wordsworth. But this beauty is a mere pale garden next to the beauty of a heart opened through suffering and sympathy, or the beauty of a mind tuned through reflection and deep thought. The experience of nature was not an escape for the Romantics so much as a lesson in humanity.

What lessons can we learn from reading all the textual references to gardens in the Word, and from being assured there are exquisite gardens in heaven, even if we can only imagine them, and then only from what we know of earthly gardens, which apparently cannot be compared to them? What do we make of the gardens of the past, or our own gardens? What do we make of correspondences, especially the lost knowledge of the living experience of them? We make what we can. We speculate and play, plant ideas and see what grows. Above all, we remain humble to the probability that we are off-track, but perhaps headed in a promising direction. We may have a sense of what a particular vine means in a given passage of the Old Testament, but what about in another passage? Does it mean anything to plant that same vine in our garden, whether we think we know what it means or not? Are correspondences things, ideas, or effects? Since the 'New Church', as described by Swedenborg, is not to be a representative church, are we misplacing energy when we attempt to create, or simply read, correspondences in our gardens?

When vexed by questions, we can return to the touchstone of use. If interest in correspondences keeps our thought elevated and open, then we are probably headed towards something good. If we want to plant certain things in certain combinations because such arrangements remind us of spiritual ideas, or God's artistry, then perhaps that effort is useful as long as we do not become fixed more on our own constructs than on the life flowing through them. Whether we plant and tend our own gardens, visit other people's gardens, or even just think abstractly about the possible meanings of plants, an essential value is to become increasingly sensitive to the power of spiritual worlds to find expression through the natural things of this world. Knowing that the worlds are interdependent is only a first step; experiencing the connection is another stride. Gardens are one of the oldest mediums on earth through which humans have tried to reflect (and reflect upon) heaven.

There is a story of a rich man who built a magnificent house on a large tract of land covered with majestic old trees. The man issued standing orders that should the house ever catch fire the trees immediately surrounding the house were to be hosed down with water before any attention was given to the house. He made a priority of the trees that had been growing patiently for hundreds of years, long before he built a lavish dwelling. In our own lives we need to issue standing orders to protect the things we value, especially those things that bear witness to a far more impressive reality than the enclosed, sometimes gaudy realm of our own ego. If we see the physical world as a theatre for the Divine and look for meanings and inspiration, whether we plant actual gardens or not, we can become spiritual gardeners, learning to care for and value this natural world as the footstool of heaven, thus preparing for a homecoming beautiful beyond words.

Endnotes

Introduction

[1] The word 'correspondence' is used throughout this essay in a specifically Swedenborgian sense to mean an object, word or image connecting the physical world to a spiritual realm of meaning and first causes. For further information about Swedenborg's idea of correspondence and the influence of this idea on later writers and periods see Jonathan S Rose, Stuart Shotwell and Mary Lou Bertucci (eds.), *Scribe of Heaven: Swedenborg's Life, Work, and Impact* (West Chester, PA: Swedenborg Foundation, 2005).

[2] For a list of major biographical treatments of Swedenborg, see David B Eller, 'Recommended Works', in Jonathan S Rose et. al. (eds.), *Scribe of Heaven*, pp. 377-9. Also useful are Robin Larsen (ed.), *Emanuel Swedenborg: A Continuing Vision* (New York: Swedenborg Foundation, 1988), a pictorial biography and anthology of essays about Swedenborg's life, times, work, and influence; and Erland J Brock (ed.), *Swedenborg and His Influence* (Bryn Athyn, PA: The Academy of the New Church, 1988), a collection of essays and papers similarly focused on the man and his influence.

[3] Swedenborg generally uses the term 'the Word' to refer to those books of the Old and New Testaments that he believed to contain an internal (or

spiritual) sense in addition to their literal sense. He lists these books in *Arcana Caelestia*, tr. John Elliott, 12 vols. (London: Swedenborg Society, 1983-99), vol. 12, §10325, p. 294. However, it must be noted that, elsewhere, Swedenborg also speaks of books in addition to this list as part of 'the Word'. See, for example, *The True Christian Religion*, tr. John Chadwick (London: Swedenborg Society, 1988), vol. 2, §§528 and 643, pp. 591-2 and 682-3, where Acts and the Epistles of Paul are, respectively, also included.

4   Emanuel Swedenborg, *Conjugial Love*, tr. John Chadwick (London: Swedenborg Society, 1996), §294.1, p. 282.

5   Stephanie Ross, *What Gardens Mean* (Chicago and London: University of Chicago Press, 1998) takes a philosophical approach to examining various definitions and characteristics of gardens; see especially her first chapter, 'Gardens and Art, Gardens as Art'. In later chapters Ross looks closely at eighteenth-century gardens and concepts of gardening, drawing connections amongst the three media of painting, poetry, and gardening.

6   Penelope Hobhouse, *The Story of Gardening* (London: Dorling Kindersley Limited, 2002), p. 19.

7   See Rae Spencer-Jones's description in *1001 Gardens You Must See Before You Die* (Hauppauge, NY: Barrons, 2007), p. 808. The book provides photographs and brief descriptions of extant Mughal gardens, as well as gardens from other areas and time periods. The book is not an historical or technical study so much as a visual guide to the variety of Eastern, Middle Eastern, and Western gardens.

8   See Swedenborg, *Arcana Caelestia*, vol. 1, §540, p. 189. Swedenborg describes newcomers to the spiritual world as needing to be disabused of their shallow views that heaven is some eternal paradise of endless feasting, conversing, and praising God. The opening passages of Swedenborg's *Conjugial Love* describe six groups of newcomers and their misconceptions

about heaven and spiritual life. The fourth group (see §3.4, p. 3) cling to the notion that heaven provides a literal return to the fruits and flowers of Eden. A steady and cloying diet of this way of thinking, however, helps them recognize their conception as prison not paradise.

9 Swedenborg, *Arcana Caelestia*, vol. 2, §1588, p. 197.

10 Ibid., p. 193.

11 Swedenborg uses the term 'most ancient' to describe early people living in a prelapsarian state of direct communication with heaven. His concept of most ancient and ancient people aligns with the classical concept of golden and silver ages.

12 Swedenborg, *Arcana Caelestia*, vol. 2, §1122, p. 6.

13 Ibid., §1622.2, p. 213.

14 Ibid., §1622, pp. 212-13.

15 Ibid., §1588, p. 197. Emphasis added.

16 Ibid., vol. 5, §3942, p. 233.

17 The term 'conjugial' here is Swedenborg's word for married love. In *Conjugial Love*, §65, p. 69, Swedenborg describes this love as the fundamental love which originates from the marriage between good and truth: 'from this marriage arise all the loves which make heaven and the church present with a person'. He goes on to describe conjugial love as a union of love and wisdom.

18 Swedenborg, *Arcana Caelestia*, vol. 5, §3942, p. 233.

19 Ibid., vol. 2, §1409.1, p. 120 and §1118, p. 4.

20 R L Tafel (tr., ed. and comp.), *Documents concerning the Life and Character of Emanuel Swedenborg* (London: Swedenborg Society, 1875-7), vol. I, Doc. 5, pp. 32-3.

21 R L Tafel (tr., ed. and comp.), *Documents*, vol. II, pt. I, Doc. 251, pp. 402-3.

22 Vigen Guroian, *The Fragrance of God* (Cambridge: Wm B Eerdmans Publishing Co., 2006) explores the beauty and significance of kitchen

gardens as well as flower gardens, suggesting that it is our husbandry, humility, and cooperation with God that matters more than the nature of the produce.

[23] See Stephanie Ross, *What Gardens Mean*, pp. 25-48, for a discussion of French formal gardens and English landscape gardens.

[24] Swedenborg, *The Spiritual Diary*, tr. George Bush and John H Smithson (London: Swedenborg Society, 2003), vol. 3, §3916, p. 233.

[25] Swedenborg, *The True Christian Religion*, vol. 1, §208, p. 268.

[26] John Milton, *Paradise Lost*, Book IX, ll. 496-504.

[27] Swedenborg, *The True Christian Religion*, vol. 1, §231, p. 285.

Part I—Garden Correspondence

[1] Swedenborg, *The True Christian Religion*, vol. 2, §511, p. 480.

[2] Ibid., §524.3, p. 589.

[3] Swedenborg, *Arcana Caelestia*, vol. 1, §§50-1, pp. 27-9.

[4] Swedenborg describes the most ancient people as follows: 'the thoughts of the most ancient people on our planet, who were heaven-like people, were composed of correspondences themselves, and [...] all the natural components and phenomena of the world which were before their eyes enabled them to think in this way. And as this was their nature, they associated with angels and spoke with them, and it was thus, through them, that heaven was joined with the world. That is why this period was called the Golden Age'. *Heaven and Hell*, tr. K C Ryder (London: Swedenborg Society, 2010), §115, pp. 77-8.

[5] Swedenborg, *Arcana Caelestia*, vol. 1, §98, pp. 27-9.

[6] Ibid., §122, p. 52.

[7] Augustine, *The Literal Meaning of Genesis* (Book 8, Chapter 10.18), quoted in Guroian, *The Fragrance of God*, p. 63.

[8] Swedenborg, *Arcana Caelestia*, vol. 1, §345, p. 122.

9 Ibid., §305, p. 109.

10 Robert Pogue Harrison, *Gardens: An Essay on the Human Condition* (Chicago and London: University of Chicago Press, 2008) describes the unattractive nature of a passive Eden, insisting instead that Adam and Eve needed to become cultivators and givers, not just consumers and receivers. See especially Chapter One 'The Vocation of Care', pp. 1-13.

11 Swedenborg, *Arcana Caelestia*, vol. 12, §10669, pp. 503-4.

12 Swedenborg, *Apocalypse Explained*, tr. John C Ager, rev. John Whitehead (Bryn Athyn, PA: Swedenborg Foundation, 1995), vol. 4, §739.8, p. 623.

13 Swedenborg, *Arcana Caelestia*, vol. 2, §1588, p. 197.

14 Ibid., vol. 10, §8326, pp. 132-3.

15 Swedenborg, *The True Christian Religion*, vol. 2, §687.2, p. 728.

16 Ibid., §695.6, p. 746.

17 Swedenborg, *Arcana Caelestia*, vol. 7, §5116.5, pp. 101-2.

18 Ibid., vol. 4, §3000, p. 54.

19 Ibid., vol. 1, §1069, pp. 449-50.

20 Ibid., vol. 12, §10669.4, p. 505.

21 Ibid., §10669.3, p. 504.

22 Swedenborg, *The Doctrine of the New Jerusalem concerning the Sacred Scripture*, [tr. Wm C Dick] (London: Swedenborg Society, 1954), §96[a], p. 105.

23 Ibid.

24 Ibid.

25 Swedenborg, *Arcana Caelestia*, vol. 2, §1772, p. 283.

26 William Blake, 'Auguries of Innocence' (1803), in *Complete Writings*, ed. Geoffrey Keynes (Oxford: Oxford University Press, 1985), p. 431.

27 Lord Alfred Tennyson, 'Flower in the Crannied Wall' (1869), in *The Poetical Works of Alfred Tennyson* (Leipzig: Bernhard Tauchnitz, 1870), vol. VI, p. 204.

28 Guroian, *The Fragrance of God*, p. 47.

29 Ibid., p. 69.

30 Swedenborg, *The True Christian Religion*, vol. 1, §230, p. 285.

31 Ibid., §231, p. 285.

Part II—Gardens in Heaven

1 Swedenborg, *Coronis*, tr. James Buss (London: Swedenborg Society, 1966), §27.3, p. 34.

2 Swedenborg, *Apocalypse Explained*, tr. John C Ager, rev. John Whitehead (West Chester, PA: Swedenborg Foundation, 1997), vol. 6, §1214.2, p. 376.

3 Ibid., §1214.2-3, p. 376.

4 Swedenborg, *Coronis*, §7, p. 17. The equation of a regenerated human with a garden is similarly underscored in *Arcana Caelestia*, vol. 10, §8326, pp. 132-3.

5 Swedenborg, *Arcana Caelestia*, vol. 2, §1624, p. 214.

6 Swedenborg, *The Spiritual Diary*, tr. W H Acton and A W Acton (London: Swedenborg Society, 2002), vol. 1, §1475, p. 433.

7 Cf. Swedenborg, *Arcana Caelestia*, vol. 7, §5116, pp. 100-2.

8 Swedenborg, *Conjugial Love*, §8, pp. 10-13.

9 Swedenborg, *Arcana Caelestia*, vol. 1, §540, p. 189.

10 Swedenborg, *The Spiritual Diary*, tr. George Bush and James Buss (London: James Speirs, 1889), vol. 4, §5174, p. 330.

11 Swedenborg, *The True Christian Religion*, vol. 1, §385.2, p. 436.

12 Swedenborg, *Apocalypse Explained*, tr. John C Ager, rev. John Whitehead (West Chester, PA: Swedenborg Foundation, 1994), vol. 5, §876.2, pp. 324-5.

13 Ibid., p. 325.

14 Ibid., vol. 6, §1211, pp. 371-2.

15 Swedenborg, *The Spiritual Diary*, vol. 1, §438, p. 141.

16 Swedenborg, *Apocalypse Explained*, vol. 5, §926, pp. 420-1.

17 Ibid., vol. 6, §1191.3, p. 336.

18 Ibid.

19 Zora Neale Hurston, *Their Eyes Were Watching God* (New York: Harper Collins, 1998), p. 182.

20 Ibid., p. 183.

21 Swedenborg, *The True Christian Religion*, vol. 1, §48, pp. 62-70.

22 Swedenborg, *The New Jerusalem and its Heavenly Doctrine*, tr. R L Tafel (London: Swedenborg Society, 1993), §24, p. 18.

23 Swedenborg, *Heaven and Hell*, §489.4, p. 390.

24 Ibid.

25 Swedenborg explains in *Heaven and Hell*, §117, p. 79, that 'Heaven's sun is the Lord, the light there is divine truth, the warmth divine goodness, both proceeding from the Lord as the sun. They are the source of everything that comes into existence and is seen in heaven'.

26 Swedenborg, *Apocalypse Explained*, vol. 6, §1211.2-3, p. 371.

27 Swedenborg, *Arcana Caelestia*, vol. 6, §4411, p. 123.

28 Swedenborg, *Conjugial Love*, §56, pp. 61-3.

29 Swedenborg, *The True Christian Religion*, vol. 1, §32.4, p. 42.

30 Swedenborg, *Conjugial Love*, §56, p. 61.

31 Swedenborg, *Conjugial Love*, §183, p. 185.

32 Ibid., §183.3, p. 186.

33 Ibid., §183.2, p. 186.

34 Ibid., §183.5, p. 187.

35 Swedenborg, *Heaven and Hell*, §241, p. 151.

36 Swedenborg uses the term *infantes* to indicate children up to five years old; see for example *The Spiritual Diary*, vol. 3, §4354, p. 385: 'an infant of five or six years old'; and *Arcana Caelestia*, vol. 12, §10225.1, pp. 206-7.

37 Swedenborg, *Conjugial Love*, §137.1, p. 141.

38 Ibid.
39 Ibid., §137.2, p. 141.
40 Ibid., §137.3, p. 142.
41 Ibid., §137.2, p. 141.
42 Ibid., §293, p. 279.
43 Swedenborg, *Arcana Caelestia*, vol. 2, §1772, p. 283.
44 Swedenborg, *Conjugial Love*, §293, p. 279.
45 Ibid.
46 Ibid., pp. 279-80.
47 Ibid., §293.5, p. 281.
48 Ibid., §294.1, p. 282.
49 Ibid.
50 Ibid., §58, p. 65.
51 Ibid., §294.2, p. 283.
52 Ibid., §316, p. 305.
53 Ibid., §316.3-4, pp. 306-7.
54 Ibid., §316.5, p. 307.
55 Ibid., §316.6, p. 308.
56 Swedenborg, *The True Christian Religion*, vol. 2, §741.2, p. 796.
57 Ibid., §741.3, p. 797.
58 Cf. Swedenborg, *Heaven and Hell*, §52, p. 31.
59 Swedenborg, *The True Christian Religion*, vol. 2, §741.3, p. 797.

Part III—Gardens in History

1 Swedenborg, *The Spiritual Diary*, vol. 3, §3578, p. 118.
2 Swedenborg, *Life in Animals and Plants*, tr. John Chadwick (London: Swedenborg Society, 2001), §40, p. 23.
3 Penelope Hobhouse's *The Story of Gardening* (2002) is an encompassing work, showing the author's passion for both sweeping historical views and

specific detail. Of particular interest, and extending outside the range of this current discussion, is Hobhouse's time chart of major gardens and developments from 3000 BCE to 2000 CE in the four geographic locations of 'Near and Middle East and India'; 'Far East' (China and Japan); 'Europe'; and 'The Americas' (pp. 12-15).

4 Hobhouse, *The Story of Gardening*, p. 18.

5 Ibid., p. 19.

6 See Exodus 4.4 for the story of Moses lifting up the serpent. In *Arcana Caelestia*, vol. 9, §6952, pp. 150-2, Swedenborg discusses the spiritual meaning of the Exodus passage.

7 Swedenborg, *Conjugial Love*, §17.2-3, p. 24.

8 Swedenborg, *Spiritual Experiences*, tr. J Durban Odhner (Bryn Athyn, PA: General Church of the New Jerusalem, 1998), vol. 1, §301, p. 294.

9 Swedenborg, *Spiritual Experiences*, tr. J Durban Odhner (Bryn Athyn, PA: General Church of the New Jerusalem, 1999), vol. 2, §3097, p. 643.

10 Swedenborg, *Apocalypse Explained*, vol. 6, §1191.2, p. 336.

11 Hobhouse, *The Story of Gardening*, p. 19.

12 Rose Standish Nichols, *English Pleasure Gardens* (New York: Macmillan, 1902; repr. 1925), p. 6.

13 Jane M H Bigelow, 'Ancient Egyptian Gardens', in *The Ostracon*, vol. II:I, Spring 2000, p. 7.

14 M A Zahran and A J Willis, 'The History of the Vegetation: Its Salient Features and Future Study', in *The Vegetation of Egypt* (London: Chapman & Hall, 1992), pp. 370-5, quoted in Bigelow, 'Ancient Egyptian Gardens', p. 7.

15 Bigelow, 'Ancient Egyptian Gardens', pp. 8-9.

16 Gay Robins, *Women in Ancient Egypt* (London: British Museum Press, 1993), p. 83, quoted in Bigelow, 'Ancient Egyptian Gardens', p. 9.

17 Edward Hyams, *A History of Gardens and Gardening* (New York: Paddington Press, 1971), pp. 13-15.

18 Swedenborg, *Divine Providence*, tr. Wm C Dick and E J Pulsford (London: Swedenborg Society, 1988), §255.2, p. 196.

19 Swedenborg, *The True Christian Religion*, vol. 2, §635, pp. 675-6.

20 Swedenborg, *The Spiritual Diary*, vol. 1, p. 16.

21 Hobhouse, *The Story of Gardening*, p. 21.

22 Leonidas Le Cenci Hamilton, *Ishtar and Izdubar: The Epic of Babylon* (London and New York: W H Allen & Co., 1884), p. 132, quoted from <http://sacred-texts.com/ane/iai/iai43.htm>.

23 Quoted in Hobhouse, *The Story of Gardening*, p. 25.

24 Hobhouse, *The Story of Gardening*, p. 29.

25 Ibid., p. 32.

26 Ibid., p. 38.

27 For background on philosophical debate in ancient gardens, see the discussion of Socrates and Plato in Robert Pogue Harrison, *Gardens: An Essay on the Human Condition*, ch. 6 'Academos', pp. 59-70, and ch. 7, 'The Garden School of Epicurus', pp. 71-82.

28 Harrison, *Gardens: An Essay on the Human Condition*, pp. 100-1.

29 Early on, Romans did have small domestic gardens adjacent to the home and devoted primarily to fruit, vegetables, and herbs. Gradually these gardens became more integrated with the architecture of the home as they were pulled into the interior to form 'peristyle' gardens, as Hobhouse describes them, which were areas for walking or reflection, with flowers, a fountain, and perhaps a pool: Hobhouse, *The Story of Gardening*, p. 143. But since these smaller interior gardens in Roman households were not discovered until the eighteenth century with the unearthing of Pompeii and Herculaneum, cities that had been simultaneously destroyed and miraculously preserved by the rivers of lava from the eruption of Vesuvius in 79 CE, it was rather the vast and stately gardens of the empire that carried Rome's influence into garden design in the Renaissance.

30 Hobhouse, *The Story of Gardening*, pp. 48-9.

31 Nichols, *English Pleasure Gardens*, p. 18.

32 Seneca, *Epistles*, 122, quoted in Nichols, *English Pleasure Gardens*, p. 20.

33 Pope's poem 'Epistle IV: To Richard Boyle, Earl of Burlington' (1731), from *Moral Essays, in Four Epistles to Several Persons*, in *The Works of Alexander Pope* (London: J and P Knapton, 1754), vol. III, condemns slavish imitation, praising instead sense, restraint, and attention to context.

34 Hobhouse, *The Story of Gardening*, p. 59.

35 Ibid., p. 60.

36 Spencer-Jones, *1001 Gardens You Must See Before You Die*, p. 802.

37 Ibid., p. 805.

38 Ibid., p. 809.

39 Ibid., p. 814.

40 Ibid., p. 815.

41 Jennifer L Leonard, 'Western Gardens at a Glance', in *Chrysalis*, vol. II, no. 2, Summer 1987, p. 112.

42 Three very useful sources for information about Islamic Gardens are: Emma Clark, *The Art of the Islamic Garden* (Ramsbury: Crowood Press, 2004); D Fairchild Ruggles, *Islamic Gardens and Landscapes* (Philadelphia, PA: University of Pennsylvania Press, 2007); and Mehdi Khansari, *The Persian Garden: Echoes of Paradise* (Washington DC: Mage Publishers, 1998).

43 Hobhouse, *The Story of Gardening*, p. 100.

44 Nichols, *English Pleasure Gardens*, p. 46.

45 Ibid.

46 Louis de Blois (1506-66), abbot of Liessies, quoted in Hobhouse, *The Story of Gardening*, p. 114.

47 Nichols, *English Pleasure Gardens*, pp. 53-4.

48 Quoted in Scott J Tilden, *The Glory of Gardens: 2,000 Years of Writing on Garden Design* (New York: Harry N Abrams, Inc., 2006), p. 91.

49 Ibid.

50 Wharton is here addressing the Italian garden. The English garden of this same time period experienced a more abrupt transition as a result of the dissolution of monasteries (and their gardens) under Henry VIII and the separation from Rome. For details about the development of Tudor, Elizabethan, and Stuart gardens in the sixteenth and seventeenth centuries, see Nichols, *English Pleasure Gardens*, pp. 101-97.

51 Hobhouse, *The Story of Gardening*, p. 116.

52 Nichols, *English Pleasure Gardens*, pp. 85-6.

53 Hobhouse, *The Story of Gardening*, p. 116.

54 Ibid., p. 121.

55 Ibid., p. 124.

56 Ibid., p. 125.

57 After studying 80 Italian Renaissance gardens and analysing their enduring appeal, Edith Wharton described this underlying harmony as a reliance on marble, water, and perennial verdure that maintained charm independent of seasons; a triple concern for matching the garden to the house, providing space for exercise, conversation, and relaxation, and adapting the garden to the landscape; and finally, the balancing of parts—converging lines of long ilex walks, alternation of sunny open spaces with cool woodland shade, proportion between terrace and bowling green, or between the height of a wall and the width of a path, and the relation of the whole to the scene about it: Tilden, *The Glory of Gardens*, p. 91.

58 Tilden, *The Glory of Gardens*, p. 79.

59 René-Louis Girardin, *De la Composition des paysages* (1777), quoted in Tilden, *The Glory of Gardens*, p. 79.

60 Abbé Jacques de Lille, *The Garden* (1782), quoted in Tilden, *The Glory of Gardens*, pp. 21-4.

61 Swedenborg, *Continuation of the Last Judgment*, in *The Last Judgment*, tr. John Chadwick (London: Swedenborg Society, 1992), §60, p. 147; *The Spiritual Diary*, tr. James Buss (London: James Speirs, 1902), vol. 5, §5980, pp. 135-6.

62 Oliver Goldsmith, *The Deserted Village*, 2nd edn. (Dublin: Printed for H Saunders, B Grierson, J Potts et al., 1770), p. 20, ll. 299-308.

63 The Romantics resisted the over privileging of reason and intellect by celebrating nature and human affection. Contemplation of a humble flower or hedge could restore health to a weary or troubled mind, but more importantly, the poetic recollection of a natural scene and one's former self could bring spiritual healing.

64 Two useful books on the history of print are: James Raven, *The Business of Books: Booksellers and the English Book Trade 1450-1850* (New Haven and London: Yale University Press, 2007); and Adrian Johns, *The Nature of the Book* (Chicago: Chicago University Press, 1988).

65 Swedenborg, *Continuation on the Last Judgment*, §§20, 40, pp. 123-4, 133-4.

66 Although most of his theology was published in Latin, Swedenborg paid for two volumes to be translated into English and published simultaneously with the Latin originals: the second volume of *Arcana Coelestia*—issued in six parts as *Arcana Caelestia: or, Heavenly Secrets*, tr. John Marchant (London: John Lewis, 1750); and *A Brief Exposition of the Doctrine of the New Church*, tr. John Marchant (London: M Lewis, 1769). *A Theosophic Lucubration on the Nature of Influx, as it respects the Communication and Operations of Soul and Body*, tr. Thomas Hartley (London: M Lewis, 1770) was translated and published with Swedenborg's knowledge, but paid for by William Cookworthy.

[67] R L Tafel (tr., ed. and comp.), *Documents*, vol. II, pt. I, pp. 549, 578.

[68] Hobhouse, *The Story of Gardening*, p. 169.

[69] On numerous occasions Swedenborg speaks of conducting 'experiments', of 'methods of testing', or of 'experiences' that read like experiments. See, for example: *Conjugial Love*, §326.4, pp. 317-18; *Heaven and Hell*, §527, pp. 427-8; and *Divine Love and Wisdom*, tr. Clifford Harley and Doris Harley (London: Swedenborg Society, 1987), §344, pp. 145-6. The style of argumentation Swedenborg uses is known as 'geometrical' after the propositional style of Euclid's geometry: George F Dole, 'Translator's Preface', in Swedenborg, *Divine Providence*, tr. George F Dole (West Chester, PA: Swedenborg Foundation, 2003), p. 5 n. 12. Even the sequentially numbered paragraphs that Swedenborg uses are a holdover from his own practice, in earlier anatomical works, adopted from the custom of some scientific and philosophical writers of the day.

[70] Swedenborg, *Arcana Caelestia*, vol. 1, §68, p. 35.

[71] For more on Swedenborg's life and works, see Lars Bergquist, *Swedenborg's Secret* (London: Swedenborg Society, 2005); Ernst Benz, *Emanuel Swedenborg: Visionary Savant in the Age of Reason*, tr. Nicholas Goodrick-Clarke (West Chester, PA: Swedenborg Foundation, 2002); Cyriel Odhner Sigstedt, *The Swedenborg Epic* (London: Swedenborg Society, 1981); and Jonathan S Rose et. al. (eds.), *Scribe of Heaven*, pp. 371-9.

[72] See Cyriel Odhner Sigstedt, *The Swedenborg Epic*, ch. 28 'Green Things Growing', pp. 237-45. Also useful is Olle Hjern, 'Swedenborg in Stockholm', in Robin Larsen (ed.), *Emanuel Swedenborg: A Continuing Vision*, pp. 319-33; and Vera Glenn, *Heaven in a Wildflower* (West Chester, PA: Chrysalis Books, 2000), especially the chapter 'Swedenborg's Heavenly Gardens', pp. 141-58.

[73] George F Dole and Robert H Kirven, *A Scientist Explores Spirit* (New York and West Chester, PA: Swedenborg Foundation, 1992), pp. 44-5.

74 Cyriel Ljungberg Odhner, 'Swedenborg's Hobby', in *Chrysalis*, vol. II, no. 2, Summer 1987, p. 158.
75 Olle Hjern, 'Swedenborg in Stockholm', p. 329.
76 Ibid., p. 328.
77 Cyriel Ljungberg Odhner, 'Swedenborg's Hobby', pp. 156-7.
78 For an extended exploration of parallels between Swedenborg's theology and his garden, see Jonathan S Rose, *Swedenborg's Garden of Theology: An Introduction to Emanuel Swedenborg's Published Theological Works* (West Chester, PA: Swedenborg Foundation, 2010).

Afterword

1 Vita Sackville-West, *More For Your Garden* (1955), quoted in Tilden, *The Glory of Gardens*, p. 143.
2 William Wordsworth, *The Prelude, or, Growth of a Poet's Mind* (1799-1805) (London: Edward Moxon, 1850), p. 371.

Appendix

Inventory of Swedenborg's Garden

1. TREES AND SHRUBS: apple; beech; berry bushes; box; buttonwood; cherry; currant; cypress; dogwood; lemon; lime; 'little tree'; mulberry; pear; 'pod bearing tree'; poplar.

2. VEGETABLES, HERBS AND FLOWERS: Allium; beets; bleeding heart; Canterbury bells (3 kinds); carrots; catmint; chalcedonica; chamomile; crown artichokes; cucumbers; flax; gillyflowers; hyacinths; larkspur; lilac; lilies; long-stemmed pinks; maize (2 kinds); marsh mallow; melons; mulberry; other bulbs; parsley; peas; rose mallow; roses (Adonis); roses (African); roses (blue); roses (sweet-smelling white); roses (velvet); scabiosa; scarlet sage; spinach; spurrey stocks; sunflowers; sweet peas; sweet william; tulips; violets.

3. STRUCTURES: arched gate; aviary; covered mirrors; covered walkway (or arbour); fences; lattice-work gazebo; maze; orangerie; root cellar; square boxes; summer house; tool shed; topiaries; walks (avenues).

4. BIRDS: doves; singing birds.

These lists have been drawn from the following sources:
Anteckningar i Swedenborgs almanacka för år 1752, ed. Alfred Stroh (Stockholm: Systrana Lundbergs Tryckeri, 1903).

Odhner, Cyriel Ljungberg, 'Swedenborg's Hobby', in *New Church Life*, vol. 43, no. 2, February 1923, pp. 65-72; repr. in *Chrysalis*, vol. II, no. 2, Summer 1987, pp. 155-61.

Sigstedt, Cyriel Odhner, *The Swedenborg Epic* (London: Swedenborg Society, 1981), ch. 28 'Green Things Growing', pp. 237-45.

Tafel, R L, (tr., ed. and comp.), *Documents concerning the Life and Character of Emanuel Swedenborg*, 3 vols. (London: Swedenborg Society, 1875-7), vol. I, Doc. 5, pp. 32-3; vol. I, Doc. 140, pp. 390-2; vol. II, pt. I, Doc. 213, p. 226; vol. II, pt. I, Doc. 219, pp. 234-5; vol. II, pt. II, Doc. 292, pp. 726-35.

Select Bibliography

Acton, Alfred (tr. and ed.), *The Letters and Memorials of Emanuel Sweden-borg*, 2 vols. (Bryn Athyn, PA: Swedenborg Scientific Association, 1948-55).

Bacon, Sir Francis, 'Of Gardens', in *The Essayes or Counsels, Civill and Morall*, ed. Michael Kiernan (Cambridge, MA: Harvard University Press, 1985), pp. 139-45.

Benz, Ernst, *Emanuel Swedenborg: Visionary Savant in the Age of Reason*, tr. Nicholas Goodrick-Clarke (West Chester, PA: Swedenborg Foundation, 2002).

Bergquist, Lars, *Swedenborg's Secret* (London: Swedenborg Society, 2005).

Bigelow, Jane M H, 'Ancient Egyptian Gardens', in *The Ostracon*, vol. II:I, Spring 2000, pp. 7-11.

Blake, William, 'Auguries of Innocence' (1803), in *Complete Writings*, ed. Geoffrey Keynes (Oxford: Oxford University Press, 1985).

Brock, Erland J (ed.), *Swedenborg and His Influence* (Bryn Athyn, PA: The Academy of the New Church, 1988).

Chadwick, John and Jonathan S Rose (eds.), *A Lexicon to the Latin Text of the Theological Writings of Emanuel Swedenborg (1688-1772)* (London: Swedenborg Society, 2008).

Clark, Emma, *The Art of the Islamic Garden* (Ramsbury: Crowood Press, 2004).

Coffin, David R, *The English Garden: Meditation and Memorial* (Princeton: Princeton University Press, 1994).

Comito, Terry, *The Idea of the Garden in the Renaissance* (New Jersey: Rutgers University Press, 1978).

Dole, George F, 'Translator's Preface', in Swedenborg, *Divine Providence*, tr. George F Dole (West Chester, PA: Swedenborg Foundation, 2003).

Dole, George F and Robert H Kirven, *A Scientist Explores Spirit* (New York and West Chester, PA: Swedenborg Foundation, 1992).

Farber, Paul Lawrence, *Finding Order in Nature: The Naturalist Tradition from Linnaeus to E. O. Wilson* (Baltimore, MD: The Johns Hopkins University Press, 2000).

Glenn, Vera, *Heaven in a Wildflower* (West Chester, PA: Chrysalis Books, 2000).

Goldsmith, Oliver, *The Deserted Village*, 2nd edn. (Dublin: Printed for H Saunders, B Grierson, J Potts et al., 1770).

Guroian, Vigen, *The Fragrance of God* (Cambridge: Wm. B Eerdmans Publishing Co., 2006).

Hamilton, Leonidas Le Cenci, *Ishtar and Izdubar: The Epic of Babylon* (London and New York: W H Allen & Co., 1884).

Harrison, Robert Pogue, *Gardens: An Essay on the Human Condition* (Chicago and London: Chicago University Press, 2008).

Hjern, Olle, 'Swedenborg in Stockholm', in Robin Larsen (ed.), *Emanuel Swedenborg: A Continuing Vision* (New York: Swedenborg Foundation, 1988).

Hobhouse, Penelope, *The Story of Gardening* (London: Dorling Kindersley Limited, 2002).

Hurston, Zora Neale, *Their Eyes Were Watching God* (New York: Harper Collins, 1998).

Hyams, Edward, *A History of Gardens and Gardening* (New York: Paddington Press, 1971).

Johns, Adrian, *The Nature of the Book* (Chicago: Chicago University Press, 1988).

Khansari, Mehdi, *The Persian Garden: Echoes of Paradise* (Washington DC: Mage Publishers, 1998).

Larsen, Robin (ed.), *Emanuel Swedenborg: A Continuing Vision* (New York: Swedenborg Foundation,1988).

Leonard, Jennifer L, 'Western Gardens at a Glance', in *Chrysalis*, vol. II, no. 2, Summer 1987, pp. 112-13.

Milton, John, *Paradise Lost*, Book IX, ll. 496-504.

Mosser, Monique and Georges Teyssot (eds.), *The History of Garden Design: The Western Tradition from the Renaissance to the Present Day* (London: Thames & Hudson, 1991).

Nichols, Rose Standish, *English Pleasure Gardens* (New York: Macmillan, 1902; repr. 1925).

Odhner, Cyriel Ljungberg, 'Swedenborg's Hobby', in *Chrysalis*, vol. II, no. 2, Summer 1987, pp. 155-61.

Pope, Alexander, 'Epistle IV: To Richard Boyle, Earl of Burlington' (1731), from *Moral Essays, in Four Epistles to Several Persons*, in *The Works of Alexander Pope* (London: J and P Knapton, 1754), vol. III.

Raven, James, *The Business of Books: Booksellers and the English Book Trade 1450-1850* (New Haven and London: Yale University Press, 2007).

Robins, Gay, *Women in Ancient Egypt* (London: British Museum Press, 1993).

Rose, Jonathan S, *Swedenborg's Garden of Theology: An Introduction to Emanuel Swedenborg's Published Theological Works* (West Chester, PA: Swedenborg Foundation, 2010).

Rose, Jonathan S, Stuart Shotwell and Mary Lou Bertucci (eds.), *Scribe of Heaven: Swedenborg's Life, Work, and Impact* (West Chester, PA: Swedenborg Foundation, 2005).

Ross, Stephanie, *What Gardens Mean* (Chicago and London: The University of Chicago Press, 1998).

Ruggles, D Fairchild, *Islamic Gardens and Landscapes* (Philadelphia, PA: University of Pennsylvania Press, 2007).

Sigstedt, Cyriel Odhner, *The Swedenborg Epic* (London: Swedenborg Society, 1981).

Spencer-Jones, Rae (ed.), *1001 Gardens You Must See Before You Die.* (Hauppauge, NY: Barrons, 2007).

Swedenborg, Emanuel, *Apocalypse Explained*, tr. John C Ager, rev. John Whitehead, 6 vols. (Bryn Athyn, PA: Swedenborg Foundation, 1994-7).

———, *Arcana Caelestia*, tr. John Elliott, 12 vols. (London: Swedenborg Society, 1983-99).

———, *Conjugial Love*, tr. John Chadwick (London: Swedenborg Society, 1996).

———, *Continuation on the Last Judgment*, in *The Last Judgment*, tr. John Chadwick (London: Swedenborg Society, 1992).

———, *Coronis*, tr. James Buss (London: Swedenborg Society, 1966).

———, *Divine Love and Wisdom*, tr. Clifford Harley and Doris Harley (London: Swedenborg Society, 1987).

———, *Divine Providence*, tr. Wm C Dick and E J Pulsford (London: Swedenborg Society, 1988).

———, *The Doctrine of the New Jerusalem concerning the Sacred Scripture*, [tr. Wm C Dick] (London: Swedenborg Society, 1954).

———, *Heaven and Hell*, tr. K C Ryder (London: Swedenborg Society, 2010).

———, *Life in Animals and Plants*, tr. John Chadwick (London: Swedenborg Society, 2001).

———, *The Spiritual Diary*, tr. W H Acton and A W Acton (London: Swedenborg Society, 2002), vol. 1.

———, *The Spiritual Diary*, tr. George Bush and John H Smithson (London: Swedenborg Society, 2003), vol. 3.

———, *The Spiritual Diary*, tr. George Bush and James Buss (London: James Speirs, 1889), vol. 4.

———, *The Spiritual Diary*, tr. James Buss (London: James Speirs, 1902), vol. 5.

———, *Spiritual Experiences*, tr. J Durban Odhner (Bryn Athyn, PA: General Church of the New Jerusalem, 1998-9), vols. 1-2.

———, *The True Christian Religion*, tr. John Chadwick, 2 vols. (London: Swedenborg Society, 1988).

Tafel, R L, (tr., ed. and comp.), *Documents concerning the Life and Character of Emanuel Swedenborg*, 3 vols. (London: Swedenborg Society, 1875-7).

Tennyson, Lord Alfred, 'Flower in the Crannied Wall' (1869), in *The Poetical Works of Alfred Tennyson* (Leipzig: Bernhard Tauchnitz, 1870), vol. VI.

Tilden, Scott J, *The Glory of Gardens: 2,000 Years of Writing on Garden Design* (New York: Harry N Abrams, Inc., 2006).

Wilkinson, Alix, *The Garden in Ancient Egypt* (London: The Rubicon Press, 1998).

———, 'Gardens in Ancient Egypt: Their Locations and Symbolism', in *Journal of Garden History*, 10 (1990), pp. 199-208.

Worcester, William L, *The Language of Parable: A Key to the Bible* (New York: Swedenborg Foundation, 1892; 10th printing 1984).

Wordsworth, William, *The Prelude, or, Growth of a Poet's Mind* (1799-1805) (London: Edward Moxon, 1850).

Zahran, M A, and A J Willis, 'The History of the Vegetation: Its Salient Features and Future Study', in *The Vegetation of Egypt* (London: Chapman & Hall, 1992).

Index

Abel, 5
Adam, xxvii, xxviii
aesthetics, xvii, xxiv, xxvi, 22, 52, 67, 70,
    79; *see also* beauty
affections, xvi, 18, 30, 50-1
Alhambra palace, 67
allegorical gardens, 72-4
alliums, 84
ancients, ancient people, xxii, 9, 57;
    ancient Egyptians, 56, 57; *see also*
    most ancients
Andramandoni, 28, 30-3, 34
angels, xvi, xvii, xviii, xix, xx, xxv, xxvii,
    5, 8, 10, 13, 14, 17, 18, 20, 21, 22, 23,
    24, 27, 28, 29, 30, 31, 32, 33, 35, 36,
    39, 40, 42, 44, 50, 54
animals, 23, 24, 42, 57, 61, 73, 82
aqueducts, 64, 67; *see also* canals
Aristotle, 62
art, xvii, 25, 35, 53, 56, 62, 68, 69, 70, 72,
    73, 74, 75, 81
artichokes, 84

Assyrians, 55, 61
astrology, 68
Augustine of Canterbury, 70
Augustine of Hippo, 5, 13

Babylonian(s), 59, 61
Bagh-e Doulatabad, 67
Bagh-e Fin, 67
Bagh-i-Babur, xviii
Bagh-i Hayat Bakhsh, 68
Bastille, 77
beauty, xix, xx, xxvi, 4, 9, 11, 12, 14, 17,
    22, 23, 25, 27, 31, 38, 41, 45, 51, 53,
    54, 55, 56, 59, 61, 62, 66, 67, 68, 70,
    71, 73, 75, 77, 85, 92, 93, 94, 95; *see
    also* aesthetics
beech, 84, 87
Benedictine monks, 70
Bible, the, xv, xxv, 8, 58; biblical, 59;
    Genesis, 2, 4, 6, 7, 58; Ezekiel, 58;
    Isaiah, 10; John, 13; New Testament,
    13, 72; Old Testament, xviii, 13, 58,